Walt's People: Volume 1

Other Books by Didier Ghez

Disney's Grand Tour (2013)

Disneyland Paris: From Sketch to Reality (2002)

Edited by Didier Ghez

Walt's People: Volumes 1-13 (2005-2014)

Inside the Whimsy Works (2014)

Walt's People: Volume 1

TALKING DISNEY WITH THE
ARTISTS WHO KNEW HIM

Didier Ghez

Theme Park Press

Theme Park Press publishes its books in a variety of print and electronic formats. Some content that appears in one format may not appear in another.

Editor: Bob McLain
Layout: Artisanal Text

ISBN 979-8-89609-096-0
10 9 8 7 6 5 4 3 2 1
Printed in the United States of America

Theme Park Press | **www.ThemeParkPress.com**
Address queries to ben@themeparkpress.com

To my grandparents, Simone and Raymond Naman.
To my parents, Yvette and Bernard Ghez.
To my brother, Fabien.
And to my wife, Rita, whose happiness is my joy.

Contents

Preface to the New Edition

Ten years have elapsed since I wrote the original foreword to *Walt's People: Volume 1*. A few months after the book series was launched, my wife and I moved from Sao Paulo, Brazil, to Madrid, Spain, and eight years later to Miami, where we now live. *Walt's People: Volume 14* is about to be released and hundreds of interviews which were languishing in historians' vaults are now available for all to read.

The series, as well as the Disney History blog (http://disneybooks. blogspot.com), which was born in 2006, are at the center of a massive effort to preserve and share Disney history while there is still time.

I am proud of what has been achieved, but there is much more to be done: at least twenty more volumes of *Walt's People* still to be released, an index to the whole series, and a lot of work to connect the dots.

Thankfully, I now rely on a new and extremely professional publisher, Theme Park Press, and thanks to the efforts of its owner, Bob McLain, I am able to reissue *Walt's People* in a much improved format and devoid of the obvious typos.

When working on this new version of *Walt's People*, Bob and I decided to modify as little as possible the text of the original edition. It remains mostly as it was when released in 2004...minus the typos.

Happy reading!

Didier Ghez
Coral Gables, Florida
March 2014

Preface

"Re-animate Disney research: unlock the vaults!"

The *Walt's People* project was born out of an email conversation I conducted with Disney historian Jim Korkis a few months ago. The magazine *Persistence of Vision* had not been published for years, *The "E" Ticket*'s future was uncertain, and, of course, the grandfather of them all, *Funnyworld*, had passed away 20 years ago. In summary, access to serious Disney history was becoming harder that it had ever been.

The most frustrating part of this situation was that both Jim and I knew that huge amounts of amazing material was sleeping in working cabinets of serious Disney historians, unavailable to Disney enthusiasts for lack of publishing venues. Some would surface from time to time in a book released by Hyperion, some would see the light of day in a fanzine or on a website, but this seemed to happen less and less often. In addition, what would surface was only the tip of the iceberg: Paul F. Anderson alone conducted more than 250 interviews over the years with Disney artists, most of whom are no longer with us today.

Jim had conceived the idea of a book originally called *Talking Disney* that would collect his best interviews with Disney artists. He suggested this to several publishers, but they all turned him down. They considered the potential market to be too small.

Jim's idea, however, awakened long forgotten dreams, dreams that I had of becoming a publisher of Disney history books. By doing some research on the web I realized that "print on demand" techniques now allowed these dreams to become reality.

Hence the *Walt's People* series. Its aim: to collect the best Disney interviews ever conducted, uncut and uncensored.

Key Disney historians have accepted my offer to contribute to the project, which will give us access to the source material they use for their works. Much of this material is published here, for the first time, in its entirety. I am also uncovering new or quasi-unknown material virtually every day: a forgotten interview with Woolie Reitherman, lost tapes of talks with Paul Murry, rare conversations with Al Hubbard, Jack Bradbury, and many others that I hope to release in the upcoming volumes of this series.

Please, if you are aware of little-know interviews or would like to contribute to this series with a piece of your own, contact me at didier. ghez@googlemail.com. We are looking for any submissions that can offer in-depth views of artists' careers or different perspectives on their works. Remember that artists already featured in a volume of this series can re-appear in future volumes if they discuss different projects or discuss the same projects in different ways.

We aim to include as many interviews as possible from artists who worked directly with Walt and therefore had first-hand knowledge about the history of Disney. We believe this should provide a fundamental source of information for future researchers.

While reading these testimonies, though, it is important to always keep in mind that no statement from any interview should ever be considered the absolute truth, as the interviewee might have misre-membered the facts, may have seen only part of the project described, or may have his own personal reasons for representing reality in a certain way. Hence the further importance of the various perspectives provided throughout this series.

For the sake of clarity: the *Walt's People* project's goal is not to earn money. Every time the cost of publishing one volume is recouped, the money will be reinvested in the publication of the next. Any surplus funds will be shared among the authors.

We aim to publish one volume of *Walt's People* every nine months to one year. I encourage you to check the last section of this volume to find more information about the next issue and how to become aware of its release date.

We hope that you will learn a lot through this series, even if you are already a dedicated Disney historian or enthusiast, and that it will stimulate you to pursue new, original Disney research.

Happy reading!

Didier Ghez
Sao Paulo, Brazil
July 2004

Introduction

Talk about a broad range of artists and subjects! *Walt's People: Volume 1* takes us from Rudy Ising to Joyce Carlson, from the infancy of animation to the making of theme park attractions that have become classics.

And this is exactly what we want to achieve in all the volumes of this series! Each book will have as broad a focus as possible, discussing Disney animation, Disney theme parks, and Disney comic-book history with interviews of the best artists in each of those fields, from the early 1920s to the 21st century. The *Walt's People* interviews, however, all have something in common: they are rare!

We aim to present mostly never-seen-before material, but we will also include very old interviews that have appeared in long-forgotten venues. Plus there will be in-depth pieces that have only been released on the web, so that they can be preserved in a more permanent format. Our goal is to explore the subject matter as thoroughly as can be achieved by serious Disney historians.

We have also tried to vary, as much as possible, the length and tone of each chapter, believing that there is no such thing as too long or too short an interview if it is well focused and it introduces us to new information and anecdotes.

And now, just a glimpse at what's ahead to whet your appetite...

In *Volume 1*, Rudy Ising brings us back to the 1920s and to Walt's first ventures before Mickey Mouse, discussing the invention of cel animation, the early storyboards, what Walt would have done if he had not moved from Kansas City to California, and why Rudy really left Disney.

Dave Hand explains what it was like to be at Walt's right hand in the 1930s and what chaos management meant to a director at the Studio at the time of *Snow White and the Seven Dwarfs*.

Bill Tytla and Ken Anderson give us the other side of almost the same picture: the artist's perspective on those early years.

With Jack Hannah, we take a detour through classic short cartoons' directing and the evolution of "The Duck", while meeting even stronger personalities from the Studio, including Carl Barks and Clarence "Ducky" Nash.

Salvador Dali, through the eyes of Disney Legend John Hench, brings us to the 1940s, while two of the Nine Old Men, Marc Davis and Milt

Kahl, give us complementary perspectives on feature animation and its challenges.

By then, we reach the 1950s, and are ready to discover how Harper Goff "tricked" Walt into producing *20,000 Leagues Under the Sea* and to explore how, during the following decade, Marc Davis, Mary Blair, Rolly Crump, and Joyce Carlson developed various classic Disneyland attractions with stories that involve, among others, Roy O. Disney and a rhinoceros.

Exciting stuff? So, without further ado, let's meet one of the pioneers....

Rudolf Ising (1903–1992)

Interviewed by J.B. Kaufman on August 14, 1988

Rudolf Ising is best remembered today for the many animated cartoons he produced in partnership with Hugh Harman in the 1930s, first for Warner Bros. and then for MGM, and for his subsequent solo work in the MGM cartoon department lasting into the 1940s. But Ising's animation career began with a long stint with Walt Disney in the 1920s. He was present for some of Disney's earliest animation experiments in Kansas City; for the rise and fall of Disney's fledgling Kansas City studio, Laugh-O-gram Films; and for many of the *Alice Comedies* and Oswald the Lucky Rabbit cartoons that Disney subsequently produced in Hollywood.

The following interview was recorded at Ising's home in Newport Beach, California, on Sunday, 14 August 1988, a few years before his death. In 1988, J.B. had no specific plans to write about Disney's silent career, but he did want to record this man's memories of those seminal events in animation history. Ising, with characteristic kindness, obliged, and that afternoon they talked for nearly four hours about his experiences in the 1920s. When Russell Merritt and J.B. Kaufman collaborated on *Walt in Wonderland: The Silent Films of Walt Disney* a few years later, this interview became indispensable, and they quoted extensively from it in their text.

This transcript is edited for clarity, and annotated to explain the historical context. At the time J.B. talked to him, Ising was suffering a slight speech impediment as the result of a recent stroke, and some of his words on the tape were not clear enough to be transcribed. Too, his memory occasionally fails him on chronological details—understandably, considering that this interview took place more than sixty years—and a crowded and colorful career—after the events in question. The present editing and annotation are inserted to clarify the historical record. In any case, the great value of Ising's words lies in his vivid accounts of the people he worked with, and the techniques they improvised together in what was then a fresh and exciting new medium. It's also worth noting that, unlike some animation veterans, Ising displays no rancor or recrimination toward any of his former associates. He emerges in this interview as exactly what he was: a dedicated professional, and a gentleman.

To better understand the interview that follows, it is important to summarize the chronology of events that preceded the creation of Mickey

Mouse in 1928, while reminding what key roles were played by all the people mentioned by Rudy Ising.

- In 1919, while living in Kansas City, Walt works as a commercial artist for the Pesmen-Rubin Commercial Art Studio, where he meets Ub Iwerks.

- In 1920, Walt and Ub go to work for the Kansas City Slide Company (later known as Kansas City Film Ad Company, and then United Film Ad Service).

- In 1921, Walt produces advertisements and little comic vignettes for the Newman Theater chain in a series he calls Newman's Laugh-O-grams. This short series is followed in 1922 by a series of theatrical narrative cartoons, spoofing fairy tales: the Laugh-O-grams. To produce these shorts, Walt establishes his own company and hires Ub Iwerks, Rudy Ising, Hugh Harman, Carman "Max" Maxwell, Lorey Tague, and Otto Walliman as animators, as well as Red Lyon as cameraman.

- In 1923, however, the company goes bankrupt, and Walt leaves Kansas City in July, heading towards Hollywood. In the meantime, Rudy Ising, Hugh Harman, and Carman "Max" Maxwell, out of work, try to create their own studio, Arabian Nights, buying the Laugh-O-grams equipment from investor Fred Schmeltz, who has acquired it through the bankruptcy proceedings. This effort, which includes a project involving musician Carl Stalling, is short-lived.

- Early in 1923, Walt had produced a pilot for what would become the *Alice Comedies* series, combining cartoons with a live-action little girl. In October 1923, New York distributor Margaret Winkler agreed to buy the series, and thus early in 1924 Walt starts hiring a new team of animators: in February Rollin "Ham" Hamilton, in June Ub Iwerks, in October Thurston Harper, and in June 1925 Hugh Harman and Rudy Ising. Iwerks, Harman, and Ising leave Kansas City to join him, as does Walker Harman, Hugh's brother, who becomes an inker and painter. In the mid-1920s, Hugh Harman and Rudy Ising take a short vacation from Disney to produce a second Arabian Nights cartoon.

- The defection of Rollin "Ham" Hamilton (who will later return to the Studio) late in 1926 leads to the hiring, in January 1927, of another Kansas Citian, Isadore "Friz" Freleng, who will later become one of the key directors of the Warner Bros animation studio.

- In April 1927, Walt delivers to Charles Mintz (Margaret Winkler's husband) the first of the Oswald cartoons, and, as is well known, in February 1928 all of Disney's key animators except Ub Iwerks are hired by Charles Mintz. This seminal event will lead Walt and Ub to create Mickey Mouse that same year.

- Rudy Ising, Hugh Harman, Friz Freleng, Max Maxwell, Norm Blackburn, Paul Smith, and Ham Hamilton, all of whom leave Disney at this time, become in 1929 the team behind the Looney Tunes series, which lays the foundation of the Schlesinger/Warner Bros. animation studio.

- In 1933, Hugh Harman and Rudy Ising leave Schlesinger and sign a deal with MGM in 1934 to produce a series of "Happy Harmonies". In 1937, MGM establishes its own studio headed by Fred Quimby, and fires Harman and Ising, who temporarily keep their studio open by producing the Silly Symphony *Merbabies* for Disney in 1938. Later, Quimby hires them back as employees of the new studio. At that time, Ising creates the character Barney Bear for MGM, basing the character partly on himself.

- In 1941, Hugh Harman leaves MGM and starts a studio with Disney veteran Mel Shaw, taking over Ub Iwerks' old studio in Beverly Hills. Rudy also quits MGM to join the army.

....

J.B. Kaufman: I wanted to talk to you today about your work in the silent days. Silent animation is hardly ever covered at all.

Rudy Ising: It's no good for television, which is one of the reasons.

JBK: To me it's fascinating stuff. It's where everything else came from. I'm interested in asking you some questions about your memories about that.

Okay. Go ahead.

JBK: The first thing I know about that you did in animation was to work at the Laugh-O-gram studio in Kansas City. Is that true?

Well, it was before Laugh-O-grams. I was there when we started that, but before that, Walt had a little art studio [that he] called Kay-Cee Studio.[1] He was doing sort of a newsreel insert for Newman theaters back there in Kansas City. I think we made a couple of song reels for

---

1 Disney had started this studio with Fred Harman, a fellow cartoonist at Kansas City Film Ad. Fred was Hugh Harman's older brother and later famous as the creator of the Red Ryder comic strip. He had abandoned the Kay-Cee venture by the time Rudy Ising became involved.

the organist there.[2] The only guys in the studio were Walt and myself. Red Lyon was probably also there at that time. He was the cameraman at Film Ad. Walt was working at Film Ad, too, during the day.

JBK: So you were working at night?

Yes. I would go to the studio during the day, built some of the equipment or helped Red with the stuff, but mostly it was at night. That went on for three or four months.

JBK: Now these were the reels that were made for the Newman theaters. They were, what, advertising and things like that?

Well, no, they were more like a thing that went into the newsreel. Like the police department decided to have horse police, and we called it "horsing around town". This was a sight gag, naturally funny, I guess, around that time. It was just a little incident like that, or maybe it was a little gag thing of some kind. Usually it went into the newsreels. This was in the single feature days, and the newsreel and the shorts were important as well.

JBK: So these would be like topical...

More or less, yes. We made those for a few months. We only made about three. There was the one about the police, and another one.... There would only be one insert in, sort of like the weekly news.

JBK: Well, I've got a reel of those, and I don't know whether any of them were the ones you worked on. Now were these the ones where you see a hand drawing the picture on the screen?

Some of them, yes.

JBK: Okay, I've got some of that.

What were they called?

JBK: At the head of the reel it says "Newman's Laugh-O-grams".

Those were before Laugh-O-grams, and then, when we incorporated, we decided to call it Laugh-O-grams. I guess Walt had just gotten out of the Canadian Air Force...no, it wasn't the air force, it was the Canadian Medical Corps. He'd tried to get in the United States Army, but he was too young.[3] This is World War I. So this was right after the war was over;

---

2   "Song reels" were short films made to encourage the theater audience to sing along as the theater musician(s) played a popular song. The Fleischer studio's later "Bouncing Ball" films are a well-known example.

3   Actually Disney had driven an ambulance for the Red Cross.

Walt was out of the army. He went back and opened what he called Kay-Cee Studio. Walt was living in a rooming house and working at the Film Ad. And I had to bail him out a couple of times. They wanted to make him leave the rooming house because of his rent and he wrote a couple of bad checks, I guess. The process server used to come up there—did I ever tell you about that?

JBK: No, no.

Well, it was during the day. See, by this time Walt had left the Film Ad. He still called [his studio] the Kay-Cee Studio then. It wasn't yet Laugh-O-grams. I had been working for three or four years and had saved up about a thousand dollars. I don't know how I did it, as I was on a very low salary. I was in the photographic business. At that time, I was about sixteen years old, and Walt was about eighteen or nineteen; he was about three years older.

So Walt wanted to know if I could loan him some money, and it ended up I loaned him five hundred dollars to bail him out on a couple of these things—I don't know just what the checks were for. Then, when [the studio] became Laugh-O-grams, we incorporated and sold stock. That was sold off, that's what we made those first six or eight cartoons with. Walt decided that rather than pay me back, he'd give me stock in the corporation. And he talked me into it. He was quite a salesman. But he was having a pretty hard time. And that's the way Laugh-O-grams started.

JBK: Okay. So you were in at the very beginning?

Oh, yeah.

JBK: How did you meet him? How did you get involved?

Well, I read an ad, and I thought I was a cartoonist. The ad said they wanted to pay a cartoonist to work at this studio and they would teach them to animate. So I answered it, and he [Walt] gave me the job. I don't know if anybody else ever answered or not—no pay, for a while. But that was to learn animation. When it came to that, Walt didn't know that much about animation. They just had the old Lutz book on animation at Film Ad.[4] It was very basic—at that time cartoons were pretty simple and basic. So I wanted to learn right along with Walt. But he had an idea—in fact, he wanted to be more a live-action director like D.W. Griffith. I might have been the vice-president at Laugh-O-grams,

---

4 E.G. Lutz, *Animated Cartoons: How They Are Made, Their Origin and Development* (New York: Scribner, 1920). This key text in animation history was reprinted in 1998 by Applewood Books.

I'm not sure. By that time Red Lyon had left. He'd moved to Colorado or somewhere, so I had to do all the camerawork on all the other stuff. It was just the two of us there for quite a long time.

But to get back to the [previous] story: this was up above a restaurant; we were up on the second floor, and the office was at the head of the stairs. We had these two partitioned offices. I knew Walt was having a hard time. A guy came up one day and said, "Is Mr. Dinsey"—D-I-N-S-E-Y, that was the way he pronounced it—"here?" And Walt said, "No, I don't think so." And he said, "Well, I'll be back," and went on down the stairs again. That's when Walt told me it was a process server. And sure enough it was, because the guy came back for a couple of weeks.

Walt and I were the only ones there, so he'd say, "Is Walt Dinsey here?" And if Walt was there he'd say, "No, he hasn't shown up today," or if it was me I'd do the same thing. You know, for about maybe two or three weeks. Finally, I believe it was Walt Pfeiffer that came up. Walt Pfeiffer was just a friend, not part of the company or anything. He came up, and I guess Walt Pfeiffer and Walt Disney were just talking away, looking at some drawings or visiting or something. And the guy came up, and before he had a chance to say anything, Walt Pfeiffer says, "Now listen, Walt," and so on and so on. [Laughs] The guy looked at him, and Walt said, "Yeah—I'm Walt Dinsey. But my name is Disney, not Dinsey!" [Laughter.] So that's when the guy finally found out, and he handed him the process and left. That's when I [also] found out Walt needed a check to help bail himself out. Because he had cleaning bills, and rent bills back due, and a couple of restaurant bills, I think.

A little after that was when we incorporated and became Laugh-O-grams and moved over on 31st Street—at that time we were above this restaurant on Troost Avenue.

JBK: And that was when you started making the fairy-tale films?[5]

Yes. We hired a salesman who went back to New York. We had made one or two pictures, I believe, at the time. I remember that *The Four Musicians* and *Jack and the Beanstalk*, I think, were the first couple. A guy by the

---

5 The Laugh-O-grams (as opposed to the Newman Laugh-O-grams), produced in 1921-22, were a series of six fairy tales "modernized" with gags and contemporary slang. In order, the Laugh-O-grams were *Little Red Riding Hood*, *The Four Musicians of Bremen*, *Jack and the Beanstalk*, *Goldie Locks and the Three Bears*, *Puss in Boots*, and *Cinderella*. Other productions including the Lafflets and the song reel Martha, alluded to later in the interview, were also produced during this period. Laugh-O-grams' last production before going bankrupt in 1923 was *Alice's Wonderland*, the original Alice Comedy, starring a four-year-old local girl named Virginia Davis.

name of Mace, Leslie Mace, went to New York to sell them, but nobody was interested. [However] there was an outfit called, I think, Pictorial Films.[6] They were the ones that eventually bought the five or six cartoons we made. We didn't have much money to operate on. I think we incorporated for fifteen thousand dollars. But by the time the broker took his cut, we only got about six to eight thousand dollars. So both Walt and I and a couple of the guys were still working for practically nothing for a long time.

JBK: Okay, when it was just you and Walt Disney and Red Lyon—how was it divided up? Were you and Disney both doing animation, or how did that work?

That was before celluloids and background paintings. You'd have a high skyline painting, and all the animation had to be below that skyline or whatever, where you had the pure white. The drawings were made on paper, and those were already inked and blacked in, painted. That's what I was doing to start with, ink the animation. Of course animation was pretty simple then.

When we started Laugh-O-grams, when we were trying to build a character, we made what you call model sheets. [For each character,] Walt would make a walk, and a run, and maybe the character in a front view, side view, and a back view. That was about it.

And the camera was stationary then. When you worked on a project we had a ten and an eight field, and a five field. These were all the full size, but the five field was the small one, supposedly like if you drew down to a five field. But the camera stand wouldn't do that, so we had to draw them. If you wanted a closeup, you *drew* a closeup. If you wanted a medium shot, you drew your animation in a medium shot. As I say, those were all inked on paper. At that time, I think I did the photographing all the time. Red Lyon was there long enough to build the camera stand, and I'd help him on that during the day. Walt and Red also represented Pathé News, for news events around Kansas City.

JBK: Did you use the same camera?

Yeah—[rest of answer not clear; something about the camera belonging to Film Ad and being used there during the day, then Disney and company using it at night].

---

6 This group, Pictorial Clubs, was the undoing of Laugh-O-grams. Their promised payment for the six films, on which Disney and company were depending, never materialized.

JBK: Oh, okay, but it wasn't the same camera that you used to shoot the animation?

Yes, an old Universal.

JBK: It was a Universal camera?

Yes. Now we had built a box because the Universal camera only had a two-hundred-foot magazine. So for publicity shots, we built a box that looked like a Debrie camera, as they called it at the time. One of those with the magazine. So we put some film cans together and painted the box and put the cans on it, and it looked real when we mounted it on the tripod.[7] Then we went out and we'd "shoot" with it. We used to have fun on weekends, going to Union Station, acting like—Walt would turn his cap around and pretend to make a film. People would come up and pose and say, "Where are you from?" And we'd say, "New York." [Next few words not clear; something about shooting in various places around town.] One was the Old Mill; it's one of the historical places around Kansas City. But anyway, when Red Lyon left I had to do all the camera work.

JBK: Was there any complicated part about that—was it pretty much just one frame at a time?

One frame with a hand crank.

JBK: But I mean, were there any technical things that you had to master to do that, to shoot the animation, or was it pretty much straightforward?

It was straightforward. Of course, when you animated, when you marked your drawings one, two, three, four, and so on, you could say it was a cycle. On a run, going forward, you'd say "Repeat cycle four times" or "Repeat this eight times." And the cameraman, sometimes if it was repeating a lot, would have a list. That was, you might say, the exposure sheet.

JBK: So you had some leeway to shoot it the way you saw fit?

Yes, that's right.

JBK: Well, that's interesting, because that flexibility was taken away when sound came in.

---

7 Actually the Debrie camera had a small, box-like appearance similar to that of the Universal. The fake camera Ising describes was made to look like the popular conception of a motion-picture camera, such as a Bell and Howell or a Mitchell, with the two round magazines mounted on top of the camera body.

Yes, that's right. And at that time we had to send our film to Chicago to be developed and printed. So we never knew what we had for about a week, [the time it took] to mail it there and back. After we incorporated, we bought a developing outfit, and I did all that, too.

JBK: You did a little of everything, didn't you?

Yes, and so did Walt!

JBK: I've read that on those early Laugh-O-grams, the Newman Laugh-O-grams, that showed the hand drawing the picture, there wasn't room underneath the lens for someone to actually put their hand, so there was a photograph of a hand holding a pen.

You're right, it was a photograph. But the reason for that…here's your platen, and there's the camera, about there, focused on this thing. A hand would be completely out of focus at that range. So we [had to use the hand photograph]. It also made it a little easier to move around. The drawing was made in blue pencil because blue would not photograph. We always used positive film for the negative then, because you got a better contrast.

JBK: And it was orthochromatic film, is that right?

Not just orthochromatic, but it was what they called printing stock.[8] The thing was made in a real light pencil. So you'd do a little bit of the thing and then you'd move the hand to that point, and then you'd move the thing and as you moved it, you had to ink in that line, until you'd inked it all the way through.

JBK: That's great! So that was your job?

Among other things, yes.

JBK: Did you make the drawings, too?

No, I think that kind of was Walt's territory.

---

8 Orthochromatic film, the standard film stock in use in the industry at this time, was characteristically insensitive to the blue area of the color spectrum. A drawing made in light blue pencil was essentially invisible to the camera, and the ink outline, traced over the pencil original, appeared to be drawn on a pure white background. In the mid-1920s, the industry would gradually shift to panchromatic film, which reproduced a wider range of color values. Ising's point is that he and Disney also used positive stock in their camera because it had higher contrast than standard negative stock, giving a more pleasing result with their solid black-and-white images.

JBK: Well, that is fascinating. The ones that I've got—let's see, I've got one that shows a motorist driving on rough streets, and his car is being shaken to pieces, and the idea is that the streets are in bad repair and need to be fixed....

I faintly remember that. That's been a long time ago, you know! But I know that when the Shriners came to town we would do a camel deal.[9] I remember that, and I remember the police, and I remember another one when—I think it was when the short stockings came in, and the short skirts. There was a little mosquito or a fly, holding a little telescope. I remember that one. Then we made one—[next words not clear; something about a swimming pool]. But I don't remember that one that you mentioned—maybe that was before I got there.[10]

JBK: I guess when you started producing the fairy-tale films, that was when more artists began to [be hired].

Yes, then we had a little money to expand. [Laughs] That's when Hugh Harman and Ub Iwerks came in. Ub used to work [for a small production company in Kansas City]. I guess he was making promotions and such because Ub was really a lettering man. He didn't do much animation to start with, but he'd do all the titles. You know, in any picture you'd have the spoken titles all the way through. He was a hell of a good lettering man—always with a brush.

JBK: Always with a brush, you say?

Yes, he did everything with a brush. He didn't animate with a brush, but he could have. That is where he got that beautiful swing that he had; he was great with a brush.

I met him, through Walt, because he did a couple of titles for the Newman things, I think. If there were any titles in there, Ub would have been the one to do them. Hugh Harman came in right about the start, and Lorey Tague, also. But I'm trying to think of guys who came out later and remained in the business. I can't think of any. The only ones, I believe, were Ub Iwerks, Hugh Harman, and myself. Then later

---

9 The Shriners were, and are, members of a fraternal order that grew out of the Freemasons in the 1870s. By 1920, they were known for their charitable work for children on one hand, and, on the other, for their colorful parades, which featured an Arabian theme.

10 Although I didn't realize it in 1988, the Newman reel I owned (then available on the 16mm collector's market) was the sample reel Disney had made to sell the series to Newman, before he started working with Ising; this explains why Ising didn't remember any of the material in it.

on came in [Carman "Max"] Maxwell and some of them. Maxwell had just finished high school, I think, in Kansas City. He was going to go back home to Arkansas, but he went to Kansas City State College, or something like that, in Kansas City.

Hugh Harman was going to go to West Point. He had just graduated from high school and had an appointment to take an examination for West Point. Walt talked him into [joining]. Because, I think it was before the war, Walt and Fred Harman—Hugh's brother—used to have an art studio. I don't know what it was called.[11] I knew Fred Harman, and that's the way Hugh got into the animation business. Otherwise, he would have gone to West Point; he was really interested in that at the time. Then, [when we started the Alice series in Hollywood] Walker Harman, their brother, came out. At the time [of the Laugh-O-grams] he was going to high school.

[As to] Friz Freleng [who joined all of us much later], he knew Hugh at Film Ad, and he applied there, too, for a job from that ad they had in the paper. There was also Nadine Simpson—Missakian now—you haven't heard of her. She was our secretary, but she never came out [to Los Angeles].

I think Hugh, Maxwell, and Ub Iwerks were the only ones I ever associated with Laugh-O-grams who came out [to Los Angeles]. Walt came out by himself the first year. And during the year he got a contract for the Alice cartoon [series, the pilot of which] we had made [in Kansas City]. On our own, really. That was the one with the live girl. Roy talked Walt into coming out [to Los Angeles], and we found out that he used the Alice comedy—it was called *Alice's Wonderland*—to get a distribution contract with Winkler Pictures. But the little girl who played the original Alice, the little blonde girl, [Virginia Davis], she was from Kansas City. She *lived* in Kansas City. Walt wanted her to come out because he wanted the same girl. So the parents decided [to move to California]. They had wanted to go to California anyway.

JBK: How did Virginia Davis come to be the one? How did she get involved?

Well, in the earlier days of Laugh-O-grams we also made a film, a dental film....

JBK: *Tommy Tucker's Tooth*, is that the one?

Yes. Dr. McCrum was the dentist. We interviewed quite a few children at the time, through a school. Walt and Dr. McCrum talked to the principal

---

11 As mentioned earlier, this was the origin of the Kay-Cee studio.

of the school. Dr. McCrum was a pretty well-known dentist there, and with his influence and Walt's gift for gab, they talked to the principal of the school. I'm not sure which school it was now, but it was a grade school. So they let Walt come out and interview children for this Dr. McCrum film, because we had four or five kids in it, if you remember it.

So I think she might have been one of the kids in there, possibly. But anyway, it was through that connection that we got Virginia Davis.[12]

JBK: Now when it came to these later things, like the dental films and the song reels, were you still a cameraman then?

I think I was doing all the camera work then. And animating a little bit, inbetweening—assisting, we called it—and camera work. I also did the developing and printing at the time. Somewhere along the line we got a projector, an electric one. Before that we had an old hand-cranked projector, really handy, by the way. I also think we got a Moviola, a very old one. They were fairly simple at that time. But they were electric. So that's the way we would cut our film and see our dailies. I was doing just about a little bit of everything.

JBK: Were you still using that Universal camera at that time?

Yes. In fact, after Walt came out [to Hollywood], Hugh, Maxwell, and I formed a company of our own [in Kansas City], called Arabian Nights Cartoons.

You see, Laugh-O-grams went bankrupt, and we went out to talk to a fellow named Schmeltz, who had quite a bit of stock [in Laugh-O-gram]. He owned a hardware store, and I guess he had about a three- or four-thousand dollar investment in [Laugh-O-gram] stock. He had a big warehouse and had moved all the furniture plus the camera stand, the camera, and some animation boards into it. We paid for it as we went along because Hugh was working at the Film Ad by that time. This was a period of about a year or a year and a half after Walt left. So we talked [Schmeltz] into letting us buy the equipment, and we finally ended up paying him off completely when we were out [in Los Angeles], working. Just paying him, you know, so much a week or a month. Then when we came to California, we shipped the Universal, the camera stand, and a couple of the animation boards out [to Los Angeles] and put them in storage. Our first cartoons were shot with that same Universal camera. We used it right through all the earlier stuff. In fact, later, we made it our test camera. Of course, by now we had a motor drive on it. Ub

---

12 Actually Virginia was still pre-school age but had already worked professionally as a model, and was recruited through that connection.

Iwerks also worked on it. We made one [additional Arabian Nights] film out here [in Los Angeles] called *Aladdin's Vamp*, I think. We were on vacation from Walt for a couple of weeks, and Ub, [Rollin "Ham"] Hamilton, Hugh, and myself made this one film.

JBK: No kidding. And that was, what, in the late twenties? It was before you started your own studio [in 1929]?

Yeah, it was about 1928, I guess. Then after I left Walt, I got a little room at the Olson building. I set up the [Universal] camera there and made a couple of plastic-surgery films for Dr. Updegraff up there. We did a nose operation and an ear operation, and we were supposed to do a breast-lift operation, but that's when we finally got a contract for our Looney Tunes. So we already had our camera stand, and we used it all the way through the Looney Tunes and Merrie Melodies for our black-and-white tests. All our animation tests we shot black and white, not color.[13]

JBK: So that remained your test camera all the way through?

Yes.

JBK: It served you well, didn't it?

Yes! [Laughter] Now when we came out here [in Los Angeles], with Walt, I used to do the camera work there, too.

JBK: When you came out here for the Alice films?

Yes. I did assistant animation, some animation, and the camera work. Principally the camera, the editing, and the printing. It was still black and white when we did those.

JBK: Getting back to Kansas City, were there any artists there that you thought were sort of the top artists at the studio?

No. Later when we came out [to Los Angeles] and worked for Walt, we were all animators. After Walt left Kansas City, when Hugh, Maxwell, and I made Arabian Nights cartoons, we had offices in the Wirthman Building. There was a theater in Kansas City called the Isis Theater, on 31st and Troost. That was in the Wirthman Building. Even when Walt was there, we used to preview some of our cartoons at this little theater.

---

13 This passage refers to the next phase of Ising's animation career, when he and Harman produced the first Looney Tunes and Merrie Melodies for producer Leon Schlesinger, for release through Warner Bros. After three years they parted company with Schlesinger, who continued to produce the cartoons himself.

By the way, we also made a couple of Newman song reels. Those were just done with animation and the organist played to them. We got to know this organist pretty well because we were in the same building and we'd see him every day there. He was Carl Stalling. He came in one day—in those days they used to play a sing-along [as part of the supporting program in movie theaters] and used slides with the song lyrics. And he said, "You know, I'd like to do something," and I think this was the first synchronized type of thing. We decided on the song "When You Come to the End of a Perfect Day". It was quite a nice song. We went up into the projection room of the theater. He had a pencil, and they had some old film, some that they'd junk once in a while. With that film we put together three hundred feet, I believe, for the verse and a couple of choruses. [Stalling] put it in the projector and he told the projectionist, "Now I want you to crank this through"—projectors, at that time, were hand-cranked, too. "And remember your crank." So he ran it through the projector, took the shutter off of the projector, and Carl, with a pencil, just literally pressed the film each time. From that we could tell exactly where the words came and how long they were held—"day" would be held, maybe, for so many frames, and "when you come" would be a little faster. From that we made our exposure sheets.

JBK: So you could tell by the pencil marks on the film...

Yes, you could tell by the pressure. From that we made the exposure sheets. On the final thing, we went out and shot a beautiful sunset. Then we had the words hand-lettered on paper—Maxwell did the lettering on those. We'd gotten part of a condenser that they used to use on [word not clear]. The other one was convex, and you'd put them together and it would magnify or reduce. We built a frame for that, and it would go up and down. In other words, as the music would swell, this thing would swell the lettering up and down. The song would come on, every word one at a time, and you'd hold for the beat but it would keep the beat going. That was all double-printed—we did that ourselves; and that was the song reel. Then Carl played to it because [in the theater] the projectionist ran it at exactly the same speed, so [Stalling] knew exactly what was going to happen. I think that was really the first sort of synchronization ever done, that I can think of. Later on we told Walt about it. In fact, we might have shown him the film. Carl came out and became Walt's musician when sound came in.

JBK: Well, that's great! I never heard about that.

Yes, it was Carl's idea, the pencil on the thing. He wanted to know how we could make a fairly accurate way of timing every word. Later on, we got so we didn't even need to time it. If we were using "When You Come to the End of a Perfect Day", the musician would write it down and we could break that down into frames. If it went to six-eight time or waltz time, whatever it was, we'd mark it down.

JBK: Getting back to my previous question: at the Laugh-O-grams studio, were there some artists who were sort of the lead artists, the top animators?

We didn't have that many [artists]! As I say, there was Ub, Hugh Harman, myself, and Maxwell, and we had one guy—I've forgotten his name—who was really sort of a successful commercial artist, but he did mostly the posters; we used to make a poster for each one. We also had Lorey Tague and Otto Walliman doing animation. And at first animation was—as I said, you'd trace the character off of a model sheet. That model sheet was photographed, and it was three different sizes, for close-up, medium shot, or long shot.

JBK: So it would actually be traced off the model sheet?

Yes, you would very often trace them. Ub was the one that later on got so that he started making them circular. We even did the model sheets out [in Los Angeles] when we made the Alice pictures. And Ub was the one that started breaking away from that. Other than that it was sort of a fastidious thing to trace the characters, and keep the likeness.

JBK: When you were animating did each artist do his own in-betweens?

More or less, yes. You'd more or less animate the whole scene; there wasn't such a thing as an assistant.

JBK: Okay, so would you say that it was mostly straight-ahead animation?

Yes, it was pretty much straight ahead.[14]

JBK: Do you, offhand, recall any scenes that you did that stuck in your head for any particular reason?

---

14 "Straight-ahead" animation is the practice of making all the drawings of an action, from the first to the last, in order of their appearance on screen. In later years, at the Disney studio, this practice was largely replaced by "extreme" or "pose-to-pose" animation, in which the important stages of the action were drawn first and the in-betweens were filled in afterward. This practice allowed the animator greater control over the timing of the scene.

I can remember my first one in *The Four Musicians of Bremen*, [since] it was the first one I ever animated on. There was a trunk, and in this trunk were the four musicians, and the trunk was out on the water—how it got there I've forgotten. It fell overboard or something. The dog character lassoed it and pulled it in. I animated the whole thing, the lasso, and him going out and pulling it in. When I saw that scene on the screen—you got a feeling that you'd gotten some of your life into it. That's the feeling you got out of it.

JBK: I'll bet that was really exciting.

Yes, it was. I remember that scene, very definitely. Then in another picture—I remember the king. He was eating popcorn in a theater, only he was in a box seat eating popcorn.[15] I remember crowds coming in and out of the theater. But I can't remember too much of anything else.

JBK: I know there's a lot of movie theater action in *Puss in Boots*.

Puss in Boots was another one, yes. I've forgotten just what I might have done in that, but I obviously [worked on it] because I used to animate quite a bit then.

JBK: There was a caricature in that called Rudolph Vaselino.

Yes. Valentino was a screen idol at the time. And we used to sit around and make up our own stories, so those modernized fairy tales were not much like the [original] fairy tale, usually.

JBK: Were there story conferences, or did you...?

Some of it we sort of made up because we had to get a general idea, and then we'd start drawing some scenes. But generally, we had a pretty good idea what the story was going to be. We didn't make storyboards at that time, we just went along...

JBK: You sort of talked it out?

Yeah.

JBK: I've read that the Laugh-O-grams studio also made shorter little films called Lafflets that, among other things, included some clay modeling. Did you ever get in on that?

Yes, we did some. In fact, I shot those. Ub was in one of them. He went in and made a model of Warren G. Harding. It was sort of a takeoff on him, and he was smoking a cigarette (I don't know whether Harding

---

15 This scene appears in *Puss in Boots*.

[really] smoked cigarettes or not). The Lafflets were a joke reel about timely topics of the day. We had, usually, jokes from *Judge* and *Life* magazine, and they put a bunch of them together. And some of them had matchstick animation. So we made a couple of those, and we had a character with a music box crank. He would crank the jokes, and they would come out with a laugh. The Lafflets was a series of jokes. It could be around the time we did the song reels for the Newman theater, too.

JBK: So if you were photographing these—like the ones with the clay, and those with the matchsticks—were you also manipulating them, or doing whatever it took to make them move?

No, that was Ub Iwerks. I was going to tell you how that was done. You made the model. After the model was finished, he smoked a cigarette. He had a cigarette in his mouth, and we blew the smoke with a pipe, that was shot full crank. Now what happened: the model was made, complete. Then he walked in backwards; everything was shot in reverse. He walked in backwards, but actually, when you ran it, he was walking away. He walked in to the clay model, turned around, and started just really throwing this clay. I think we did a slow crank on that [to speed up the action on screen]. When it was over, we cut to the closeups with the smoke coming out and what-not. After that was done, he just had the pile of clay and he just walked backwards off the stage. So in reverse, the whole thing was that he walked in, he dumped the thing, set it up like that, and, when he was finished, turned around and walked off.

JBK: So it looked as if he just did it instantly.

Yes, but actually he just tore it down. Sort of slowly. I believe we did a slow crank on that. Not stop motion, but a slow crank.[16] The cigarette was also done on a slow crank, but when he winked his eye, or something like that, that was done in stop motion, on the model itself. Ub was the artist on that. We also did some song reels. We used to hire models to model in these things. We made a song reel called *Martha, Just a Plain Old-Fashioned Girl*. Ub was the actor in that. Walt directed, and I shot it. We built the sets for that out in the alley at the back of the building.

---

16 "Slow crank" refers to slowing down the camera in order to speed up the action onscreen. "Stop motion" is the practice of photographing one frame at a time, the method by which all animation (miniature and clay animation as well as hand-drawn animation) was photographed.

JBK: You and some of the other people at Laugh-O-grams also appeared in the original Alice film. How did you feel about that, about seeing yourself onscreen?

Well, that wasn't the first time. We used to go out, as I say, down to the Union Depot just for entertainment. We'd go out on weekends, go out and shoot some pictures. We shot some pictures of ourselves out at Swope Park with the camera, and a still camera, too. No, we had a lot of film, we used to take pictures of ourselves quite a bit.

JBK: So you were pretty well used to it by then.

Yes, at least I was, so it didn't really make any difference.

JBK: Sounds like there was a lot of fun mixed in with the work.

Yes, those early days were really...we were learning so damn much at the time. Everything we had to learn, we were in Kansas City and every-thing was done out [in Hollywood] or in New York, where pictures were concerned. So, in a way, it was a lot of fun, yes.

JBK: When you were doing the camera work, when you wanted to do irises, did you do that with the diaphragm of the camera [lens], or was that done in some other way?[17]

We had a little iris, about that size. You moved it, then you shot a stop frame, then you moved it and gradually closed it or opened it. It was actually *like* in a camera lens. They used to use them in [live-action] pictures. They very seldom used the iris, [the actual diaphragm], in the camera, because that would [reduce the exposure and create] a fade or dissolve. With the iris, they definitely had to close a thing that was [outside the camera lens and] usually about so far away from the lens. We did the same thing; we had a little mount below the camera [as the camera pointed down at the camera table]. Let's say the camera was here, and we had a little thing that we'd slide the iris in. Because we might iris down to any part of the scene—we could do that by moving the little frame we had down. You'd have your scene, and we could move the iris

---

17 The practice of opening and closing a cartoon with an iris-in and iris-out (a circle opening and closing against a black background), common in classic animation throughout the 1930s and 1940s, had its roots in films of the silent era. The device Ising describes was called the Vignetter, and was mounted directly in front of the camera lens, enclosing the scene in a circular "frame" that was slightly out of focus and had a soft edge. As he says, the device was used to similar effect in live-action films. Later cartoon irises, which opened and closed with a hard edge, were made with a series of black cards with round cut-out openings of graduated size.

to close down on any part of it. It was like the animation boards with the pegboards where they could make pans, why, this was the same way. Same idea as moving the camera, but we would just move the little mechanical thing. You'd move that in stop motion every frame. You'd look through the aperture in the camera and it would show if you were closing down to the right point, and then that was the way you did it when you shot it. That was part of the camera equipment, I guess you would say.

JBK: So the studio [in Kansas City] folded up and then you made the *Arabian Nights* film…

Yes. Max was going, as I say, to junior college or college, I don't know which. Hugh was working at the Film Ad, after Walt [had left for California]. And I had a neighborhood [word not clear] business. I would work on that during the day, and then Hugh, Max, and I would work on this film at night.

JBK: You didn't manage to sell it?

No. We tried, but we couldn't sell it. And then we heard from Walt. He was making [the] *Alice Comedies* when we came [to join him in Hollywood]. When we left later on, Hugh and I started our own business. [Just after that Walt created] Mickey Mouse.

JBK: So you were here, [in California], for Alice and for Oswald the Rabbit?

Yes. Not for all of Oswald, but I was there for quite a few of them. But not for Mickey Mouse.

JBK: How was it different when you came out [to Los Angeles] to do the Alice films? How was it different from when you'd been doing the things in Kansas City?

Nothing [was different]. I mean, as far as our work. The new man in the organization then was Roy. We never knew Roy back in Kansas City. And Roy was the one that really talked Walt into coming to California. Walt was almost ready to go back and work for Winkler Pictures; he was trying to sell Winkler on the other cartoons we'd made. They, at the time, were releasing *Felix the Cat*—I think Bill Nolan was the animator on that, in New York. In its way, the drawing was pretty good on the old black-and-white Felix. But Walt was going to go back East and get a job; I think they'd offered him a job. He'd written them and they said, well, why don't you come back here and work on Krazy Kat cartoons or something. Roy was the one that [convinced him to move to Hollywood].

Their Uncle Robert had a house down there and a garage that he didn't use. They could live [there], and didn't have to pay board. [That's where] they got started. I think that Roy never got the proper credit for what he did to make the big Walt Disney success. He was the man that always brought in the money. He was a hell of a nice guy, that got along great with people—which included bankers and animators and in-betweeners and all that. So he should have a lot of credit for Walt's success. He was the only new person. We knew Ub and Walt. Hamilton we met when we came here, and Ham's sister used to do the painting.

JBK: Did she?

Yes, she did the painting and Walker Harman inked the whole thing, on the drawings. Then, too, you would ink the drawing, not a cel. Later on we got into using cels. But we were pretty much the same group. When we came out [to Hollywood], I think the next week Walt got married. We knew Roy and Ub, and we used to all get together nights and weekends. It was just a little closed group, so to speak. We'd go to Walt's house and they'd come to our apartment. We never went to Ub's house, because Ub had his mother living there. She did not approve of any of us, because at one of the parties Ub got drunk and she always blamed us for that.

JBK: So your method of working, then, was pretty much the same [as in Kansas City]?

Exactly the same, yes.

JBK: You still used the model sheets?

Yes, but eventually we got out of that habit, and Ub was the one that really started that. Then Walt was doing quite a bit of the animation, and he was doing the timing, too. I think we'd gotten into exposure sheets around that time. Either on the *Alice Comedies* or Oswald. For the *Alice Comedies*, we used to have to project the Alice part down to make the black outline sketches of her.

JBK: I was going to ask you about that. How was that done? Was that done all in the camera?

Alice was shot in an area that was about the size of that room [he indicates a small anteroom with a door opening roughly eight feet wide], and the canvas came down from a height of maybe ten feet. It came down and then rolled out. We had this idea back in Kansas City. Out here, we used to shoot Alice behind a billboard down on Hollywood Boulevard, in the daylight. Then we knew George Winkler, who came out and worked with his [brother-in-law]. He was a cameraman at the time.

JBK: How were the two images combined?

We got a print of her. Walt would direct her, and she would have to play a closeup or a long shot or run across the camera. Sometimes there were full shots. And we photographed her. We'd shoot about three pictures in one day. In other words, if she was a fireman, it would be [first] Alice the fireman and [then] Alice this and Alice that. We would always shoot about three at one time. Then we picked the prints we wanted, and that would be put in the [animation] camera: they had a light that went inside the camera and projected down onto a field. Then you traced the girl, you traced the area on each frame of film. Now those were never used in animation; in the final picture the girl was alive. But from that tracing we had to make what they called a traveling matte—they were filled in black on the white paper. And we shot that and got a negative made, and that was bipacked in the camera when we shot the animation. [So] it was black around her, and then the white part of her was matted out. Then when it was printed, it was double-printed, just in reverse. You used the traveling matte with the animation negative, and then you used the reverse when you double-printed her in. Sometimes, we put her negative in the camera. Some of them were done in the camera, and some not.

Later on, most of that was all done at the lab. They ran the negative to process the traveling matte, and they'd do it right on there without using the bipack. There was some grain that we got, when we'd matte in the camera. Because the matte had to be on positive film, which would eventually get scratchy. Eventually all that was done at the lab, in double printing.

JBK: Do you remember what lab it was, that was doing that? I think a few years later they were using Consolidated Labs.

That was later. No, this was another, little lab. I think it was called Producers' Lab. It was the one *we* eventually rented, after it went out of business and Consolidated took advantage and took over most of the business. Our first studio was on Hollywood Boulevard. We got too big for that and we rented the old building over on Seward Street. That's where the lab was.[18]

---

18 After the Harman-Ising studio closed in 1938, the Seward Street building entered Disney history again. Because Disney's Hyperion studio was overcrowded and the Burbank studio had not yet been built, Disney rented the Seward Street building and used it as a separate facility where much of the early work on *Bambi* was done.

JBK: By the time you came out here, you had bought out some of the equipment, including the Universal camera. And I believe Disney was using a Pathé camera then, is that right?

Yeah, a Pathé.

JBK: Was that used for both the animation and the live-action stuff?

No, they rented a regular motion picture type camera, one of the later Bell and Howells, that we used for the majority of the shooting of the little girl. Because at the same time they were doing that, very often the [Pathé] camera was being used in the studio.

JBK: Were you still doing the photography of the animation in the studio?

Yes, I think I did all the camera work on the *Alice* pictures, and the early Oswalds.

JBK: Were you still using positive stock?

For the animation part, yes. I'm trying to think when we went into negative stock. It must have been practically about the time color came in. We began using negative stock in the camera because we got a better image when we began to get into greys and backgrounds. When we were doing it with cel animation, we got into backgrounds, even in the black-and-white days. Positive stock was no good for picking up the various tones of grey, the subtle tones.

JBK: When you went from the *Alice Comedies* to Oswald the Rabbit, would you say it was easier for the staff to do something that was strictly animation, than to do the combination live-action films?

No, because by that time the lab was doing most of the printing. No, it wasn't any easier. The only thing is that [in the *Alices*] we still had to project the little girl, but other than that the animation was all the same as in Oswald, the same type of animation.

JBK: Do you remember anything about the change? I know there were three different girls who played Alice at various times.[19] Do you recall anything about how that came about, how that happened?

---

19 This was the conventional wisdom in 1988. Later, when Russell Merritt and I were working on *Walt in Wonderland*, a fourth Alice, previously overlooked by history, came to light: Lois Hardwick. The chronology of the four little actresses who played Alice is as follows: Virginia Davis, 1923-1924; Dawn O'Day (Anne Shirley), a single Alice picture in 1925; Margie Gay, 1925-1926; Lois Hardwick, 1927.

I think Virginia and her parents moved back to Kansas City or something. Or else somebody signed Virginia Davis on an exclusive contract. And then the other girl, I've forgotten her name now, but she was....

JBK: One of them was Margie Gay.

Margie Gay was a friend of one of Walt's nieces. They went to school together.

JBK: Then there was one whose professional name then was Dawn O'Day. She later changed her name to Anne Shirley when she appeared in *Anne of Green Gables*.

It could be. You see, the studio was getting to where the little group was beginning to bring in other people. Norm Blackburn and a bunch of new people started coming in. Even more so when we started the Oswald series. I think we only made thirteen *Alice Comedies* a year, and when we started the Oswalds it had to be twenty-six a year, so we had to find some new help, too.

JBK: So you had two different groups of people?

No, just more people. It got too big. Before that there was only Walt and Ub and our little group. We'd either be at their apartment...you saw them night and day, so to speak. As far as animation is concerned, there wasn't any change there, except we had to make a lot more of the Oswalds.

JBK: At the time the Oswald series started, were you still using that business of tracing the model sheets, or had you gotten away from that during the *Alice* series?

By that time I believe we had gotten away from it because Ub was developing that other style. The model sheets were still made, they were distributed to every animator, as a guide. The animators pinned it up on their animation table, but they didn't trace it any more because it limited the animation too much. If you look at some of those earlier cartoons we made in Kansas City, you'll see that every walk is exactly the same.

JBK: Do you recall whose idea it was to have a cat that looked a little like Felix in the *Alice* series?

It was probably the Winkler influence because they were distributing Felix the Cat, and they were very successful then. Have you ever seen any of the old Felix cartoons?

JBK: Just a couple.

When he had an idea he took off the top of his head and an idea came out. Or we used a balloon for the dialogue, like they still use in comic strips. The guy who was animating drew up the dialogue and it would just fade in and fade out. But we never did like the New York film ideas. If you look at the films, you'll see that we really developed a whole different type of humor than back there. Back there the things that were funny were things like some guy spits on the street, and pretty soon the character comes along and thinks it's a dime. Some of it was kind of distasteful. [For us] the story became more important at the time. So we got away from that New York type of humor. Walt didn't like it. And as I say, that could have been partly the Winkler influence, the....

JBK: There was a character that I think came in during the time the *Alice* series was being made, which Disney retained well into the thirties, and that was Pegleg Pete. Do you recall anything about that, about that character showing up in the earlier films?

No. But very often the heavy was the same type of a character, just a big guy.[20] I used to do the voice for a lot of those when we got into the sound cartoons. I was always the heavy.

JBK: Do you recall when they got into using cels rather than inking on paper?

We started that in the cartoons we made back in Kansas City, accidentally. The first time we ever got the idea, and I think it was my idea, was in *Jack and the Beanstalk*. Walt had animated, I think it was an eight-drawing cycle of the beanstalk growing. Because I don't even think we had vertical pans then, they were all horizontal, the only way our camera would work it. So that had to be an animated thing. And for some reason the beanstalk pictures all had to be cutouts, so that the character showed behind the drawings. And they were all cut—I remember, because I did it, and then glued those onto a sheet of celluloid. In effect, it became the background. And when I was cutting those, I talked to Walt about it and said, "Look, I don't know why we can't paint that on the cel instead of cutting that whole thing out," because, you know, that was a lot of work, cutting around all those leaves. And after that we began using cels a little bit more and more, for animation, for cycles, especially. But we never had the complete thing back there [in Kansas City], or even out here [in Los Angeles], we were still doing it on the paper.

-----

20 Pete had been introduced in *Alice Solves the Puzzle* (1925) and was established by the time Ising arrived in California.

JBK: Well, that's tremendous! I don't think anybody knows about that.

[Another character in the early days was Thurston Harper.] Some of the stories about Thurston Harper are pretty funny. He had a temper he couldn't control. We used to play tennis in the morning, and he would take that racket and bang it on the iron posts or on the ground, and completely ruin it, and then come over and say, "Rudy, can I borrow your racket?" He was a big, almost a perfect Jack Dempsey type of build, and a hell of a nice guy until he lost his temper. He was okay with pals and with us; he never got too rough.

One time he was animating a scene, and I was sitting next to him, and Ham on the other side. We used Eagle pencils, they were called; they were brown cedar pencils, and the lead was never exactly straight down the center. I guess they drilled through the piece of cedar and plugged the cylinder with lead or something. They were a penny apiece; that's the reason we used them. We each had a pencil sharpener and a piece of fine sandpaper. [Another thing:] Walt wasn't there, he was in the office in front with Roy. Harper had a scene I think he'd almost finished. But he would sharpen his pencil, and then he'd go to draw and pretty soon nothing, no lead, he probably got the bad pencil in the bunch. "Goddamn," and he'd sharpen the thing, have his hands clenched, and he'd go back. Pretty soon nothing was happening and "Goddammit!" He went through this about four times getting madder and madder and madder. Finally, he got up and broke the pencil in half, took the pencil sharpener and broke the thing right off the drawing board and threw it in the wastepaper basket. He took the scene that he was working on in both hands, it was almost finished, and he just tore the hell out of it, threw it in the wastebasket, got up, and walked off, like that.

Walt heard him, finally—it was only from the back door to the front door, this is when we were on Kingswell Avenue. It was all just one room when we started. The next day Harper came back in. By this time Walt knew what he'd done and he said, "I want to talk to you, Harp." Thurston said, "What about?" And he said, "You know, you're costing us too much money, we're going to have to let you go," and Harper said, "Let's talk about it out in the alley after work." There was a back door, and of course half of us used to leave out through the alley. Walt had to leave early that afternoon himself, so Harp was sitting around [laughs], at least one or two months. And Walt didn't dare, because if he'd really gone out there he knew Harper was liable to beat the hell out of him.[21]

---

21 The date of this incident is unknown, but Harper left the Disney studio at

[Harper] had some friends he used to play poker with, and he'd get a bad hand and he'd take all the cards and tear 'em in half, turn the table upside down and walk away. And if anybody gave him an argument it would end up in a fight; that happened five or six times. And *they* were good friends of his, all from Texas.

I don't know what brought that up.... You asked me something.

JBK: We were talking about the difference between using cels for some scenes and inking the others on paper.

Yeah, well, we were still using paper then. That's the reason I happened to think of that because he tore his paper right in half. Eventually, we got to using more greys in the background. And parts of the little girl we did in animation.[22] They were drawn from the figure like Walt did in *Snow White*, but just in shades of grey. But the face and everything had to be put in, and I did all the painting on those cels, that we were using then. Gradually, we evolved to a point where everything was done on cels.

JBK: So there wasn't ever a line drawn, where you used all inked paper up to one point and then cels?

No. It was a gradual development. And also a gradual development in the clarity of cels. The first cels we used to use were nothing like the later ones, which were one-thousandth of an inch or something. Those early ones were thick, and a lot of them were like plastic; plastic in various shades of clarity. You'd get several layers of them, and if you kept them through the whole scene [so the density never changed] it didn't make any difference, but if you started changing those, you'd see the difference on the screen right away. They also were very expensive. We used to wash cels; when the picture was finished, we'd wash the cels off and use them again and again and again, until they got too many pen scratches. The quality of the celluloid manufacturing [then] got better, and we gradually got to using them more and more. But for the first ones, I think we spent twenty-five cents a sheet. It was a sheet of celluloid that was, I would say offhand, two by five feet. They used to put them in a big box. I think they were made by DuPont, and DuPont actually worked with us on developing them, so the cels got thinner and thinner. But the first ones were, I would say, almost a sixteenth of an inch thick; they were pretty heavy.

---

the end of December 1925.

22 The Alice character was filmed in live action as a rule, but for intricate interactions with the animated characters, a brief bit of her action would sometimes be animated.

JBK: How about stories, at that time? Did the method of coming up with the stories evolve?

Yes. First, even in the [*Alices*], we would sit in the office and would have story meetings, Walt, Ham, Hugh, and me would all work over various gags. Walt would have an idea: let's let Alice be a fireman in this one, or let's let Alice go fishing, or whatever it was. Then we'd work up fire gags or fishing gags. I remember one of the *Alice Comedies*, I guess it was "Alice Goes Fishing". We had a dog in that, or maybe it was a cat. I know he was fishing through the ice and had a can. And the title was the old gag where you'd use a can of sardines and you put it on the edge of the ice, and when the fish comes up to grab it you'd pop him in the head.[23] Of course the original story was, if you want to go fishing in the wintertime, you have to go and get a can of peas, and when the fish come up to take a pea…. Anyway, we'd sit down and talk over the situation, come up with gags, come up with an idea of continuity, and Walt would work that out, figure out about how long a scene should be and who was the animator. Or maybe one evening when we met at his house, or our apartment, we'd also talk a story gag over. There was no story department as such, or separate story men. Eventually, as we started making more and more cartoons, we had to have a story department. Walt used to make all the early story sketches, but then it got to where Ub was making them out, and then some of them, like Hugh, would make them. During the Oswald the Rabbits, I believe we gradually started working on the storyboard idea. We'd pin up gags because we had Celotex walls for the partitions down there, and we could just use one of the partitions and put the story sketches on there.[24]

JBK: When Walt came up with Mickey Mouse after you were gone, did it seem to you that the gags that he had for Mickey Mouse were pretty much the same kind of gags that you would have used for Oswald the Rabbit?

Yes, more or less. The only difference was you'd do different things with the character. Actually, the characters themselves, even in the

---

23 It's not clear which film Ising has in mind here; the studio never made a film called *Alice Goes Fishing*. The gag he describes is roughly similar to one in *Alice's Fishy Story*, but that film was produced in April 1924, more than a year before Ising arrived in California.

24 It's important to mark a distinction between these pinned-up sketches and actual storyboards. These 1920s story drawings, some of which still survive, were made in groups of six to a page, like a comic book. The great innovation of true storyboards, introduced years later at the Disney studio, was that the sketches were all made independently and could be moved around with endless flexibility.

Alice Comedies before that, were all sort of the same basic kind of deal.

JBK: While I had the machine turned off, you were starting to tell me about the boy and girl models and the characters that were on the title frame of the Laugh-O-grams—how the same characters were used over and over.

Yes, they were used, I think, in nearly every so-called modernized fairy tale. At least the dog and the cat were. Now with the human characters, it would just depend on the story...the boy was in *Jack and the Beanstalk*, but I don't think there was any girl in that. I think we more or less, on most of them, carried the cat and dog as a running thing. But there was never a plan to do that, it just happened that way.

JBK: How did you come to leave the studio? I think you were away from the studio by the time the Oswald series was taken over and they went into Mickey Mouse.

How did I leave Walt Disney? [I had a problem with falling asleep.] It took me about three or four years to get over that sleeping problem. The change in coming from Kansas City out here, I don't know just what it was. Camera work was pretty monotonous once you started to photograph, and I used to fall asleep between frames. Then we had a motor drive—you'd pull the cord and it would click, and the motor was kind of noisy, and every once in a while I'd fall asleep. Walt told me one day, "It's too costly, if you're going to keep falling asleep." My brother had the same malady.

In those early days I was interested as much in photography as I was in being an artist. But the thing I wanted to do in photography was portraits. I was as much interested in that as I was in being an artist or a cartoonist. So actually I said, "Look, Walt, why don't I just leave, and you can get somebody else for your camera." And he said, "No, I don't want to do that," and I said, "Yeah, but I'd just as soon, why don't I leave." And that was it. He probably would have fired me if he'd caught me asleep another time, at the camera. But I left.

That's when I got into doing some portraits as an independent photographer, and also doing the animated operations, the nose job and the ear job. I also worked for a commercial artist for a little while, and for a very short time I got to work out at MGM in the still department, under Clarence Bull. I remember they were making the first *Trader Horn*. They had mailed in the stuff, and [the film] had to be developed and printed and sent back immediately, so they could tell whether they had to reshoot a thing or not. I worked out there for about a month, doing that job on *Trader Horn*. Eventually, George Winkler [Margaret Winkler's brother] came to Hugh and me. He wanted us to take over the Oswalds. He gave us a studio and we made the Oswalds for a while. Then Walt Lantz—who was working for Winkler at the time—he and Bill Nolan got the Oswald contract with Universal. That's how I left Walt Disney. No animosity, nothing like that.

JBK: When you were making the Oswalds for Winkler were they still silent?

Yes.

JBK: Would you say that anything was different, or were you still doing pretty much the same thing?

Pretty much the same. But by then we were using cels completely, no more inking the drawing. It was the same as doing them for Walt.

JBK: You had, by that time, completely got away from just tracing the model sheets?

Yes, a long time before that. That was during the *Alice* films. As I said, we had them pinned up on the animation table, but we never used them for tracing. At that time, the characters were a circle for the head and a circle for the body and four legs, and Ub's the one that dropped that type of character, too. Even Oswald changed somewhat during the time we were making the Oswalds. Ub would lay out a scene, and it made the animator's work easier. If you followed one of those, you could almost trace it because he'd lay out the whole animation scene on about three pieces of paper.

JBK: How would you describe the change in your work, as far as animation is concerned? Before the Oswald days were over, were you doing full animation yourself?

Yes, and on some of the earlier cartoons, too, but there were so many other things to be done at the time. We were making twenty-six pictures a year, so I probably got involved in the camera work and the lab work. And the same with Walt, he gradually got out of any animation, any drawing, himself. Besides that, Walt was never too much of a cartoonist, and neither was I. No, I wasn't that good. Hugh was a good animator, and good at drawing, and so was Ub, and some of the other guys. Ham was the only one I know of that couldn't follow a model sheet—he was a hell of a good animator, but he couldn't follow a model sheet. For Walt, when we were doing twenty-six pictures a year, it was a full-time job for him to lay out and do the timing, and, you know, think up stories and all that. He wasn't doing very much animation, as I recall, at the end of the Oswald pictures.

JBK: Would you have been the man who made stills for the studio at any point during this time, or *were* there stills—like 8x10 photographs of the scenes?

Yes, I did all the stills back in Kansas City. But we didn't make scene stills. They were mostly gag or advertising, we didn't use many stills.

JBK: Well, I noticed there was one there that you said was from *Martha*, with Ub Iwerks....

Oh, yes. I think Maxwell actually shot that. I think he shot that and did the camera. We had a 5x7 camera that I did a lot of still stuff with. We started an art class for a while back there. Walt thought that we should all have more of a training in art, and he got the idea of having a night class once a week, a life class.

JBK: In Kansas City?

Yes.

JBK: That's fascinating because ten years later they were doing that on Hyperion.

Well, now this life class wasn't really photographing the action or anything. No, this was just where we put an ad in the paper and had ten or fifteen gals come to answer the ad, and I photographed them. I think we only needed one or two models during that period. It didn't last too long, the life class. But anyway, there were a lot of things I had to shoot as stills. Like *Tommy Tucker's Tooth*: I did all the still work in that.

JBK: Were there any other cartoon producers that you or the group especially admired, like the Felix the Cat series and so on? Were there any of those that you liked better than others?

Well, we liked the originals. In fact, even when Walt was back in Kansas City, this girl who we had as a secretary had worked before at a couple of film exchanges. And we knew several people at the film exchanges. Universal didn't ship their film. They sold it to a guy who had the whole state of Missouri or the whole state of New York. They called it "states' rights". We knew several people down there, and they were the ones who handled the film, and they just rented it to all the theaters in Kansas City. [We would get their used prints when they discarded them;] when a print got scratched up they'd actually take it down to the city dump. Sometimes Nadine [Simpson] would go down and get a couple of the cartoons, and the ones we got mostly, then, were *Aesop's Fables*. That's because we were concerned with how they got a quick turnover. They got a lot of live film, and then of course we got some cartoons.

When Nadine would get us one of the *Aesop's Fables*, we'd run it, and we'd cut out a cycle. We'd cut out maybe a two-hundred-foot run section where Al Falfa would chase a lion—then the lion would chase him, and they'd repeat that back and forth. I'd cut out a whole repeat of the film and look at how they'd change it back. Then Nadine and I would splice it together again and put it in—everything was hand-spliced then. And we'd look at some of the timing of the animation.

But we never liked the ideas in the KoKo the Clown pictures.

JBK: Fleischer?

Fleischer, yes. We didn't like the stories. They had a lot of live shots of their studio and what-not. We figured out how they did their KoKo: they actually photographed a clown and then traced him—they traced and painted him. We were never too fond of the Fleischer cartoons. Even the Betty Boops we didn't think were that good. Oh, I guess we liked Popeye, but I don't know why. None of their cartoons ever had much of a story, and we were more interested in story cartoons than we were in character cartoons, so to speak.

JBK: So in Kansas City you probably looked at the *Aesop's Fables* more than at any other things?

In the early days, yes, [we looked] more [at the] *Aesop's Fables* because we had this girl that knew the booking office of *Aesop's Fables*. That might have been the reason. [Laughter]

After we moved [to Los Angeles], Margaret Winkler had married [Charles Mintz]. [The Winkler studio] became his studio and not hers. They were mostly in New York until he moved out here. We made the early Oswalds through him. But at the time they were working with a bunch of New York people, too, including Walt Lantz. Lantz and Bill Nolan got together, after a year or two, and that's when Walt Lantz started making the Oswald the Rabbits. He did change Oswald somewhat, gradually, because by that time we were doing more of the rounded things, rather than the pointed nose on those mice. Anyhow, he stole the whole staff away from us and decided he wanted to make them.

When we signed up with him, we were trying to get started on the *Looney Tunes*. We had made this Bosko sample reel, and showed it to Leon [Schlesinger]. He wasn't too interested. I had made a couple of animated titles for him, when he was running Pacific Title Company. But he did finance our first two cartoons. They were made for three thousand dollars each. I don't think he ever had more money than that original three thousand dollars, in advance. Warners paid him and he sent us the check, so we knew how much money we had. That's when sound had just come in, and he knew that the title business was about finished. Because up till then, about fifty per cent of his titles were the spoken cards. He and Hugh never got along, but I got along okay with him.

We continued that year, and then we went to a second series, the *Merrie Melodies*. On *Looney Tunes*, he was supposed to pay us five thousand, and he said, "No, we can't do that, you'll have to take thirty-five." We decided we couldn't do it because we had an awfully big staff then. So that's when he started his own studio. He was all right, he was just a businessman.

We had a short contact with Paul Terry, and made one or two cartoons for Van Beuren. Then Quimby decided he wanted to make cartoons, he wanted to be a producer over at MGM. And later we got in an argument with *them* and quit, and they took over. So, twice, we launched the damn thing and then left it. To Quimby and Schlesinger. But I never pushed my friends. They were strictly business. Schlesinger had to get into another phase of the picture business. Quimby, he wanted to be a cartoon producer. Before that he was a business manager at the studio, the sales head of the shorts department.

As far as other cartoon producers, we never got personally involved. Leon just went along with what we had done up to that point. The only change: he got a couple of good guys like Tex Avery and Chuck Jones. Walt Lantz we never became personal friends with. Quimby and Schlesinger continued to do the same thing we had done. Bob Allen, too. He was in story sketch, animation, and layout [in my team at MGM].[25] Bill Hanna was in my story department. He was a good story man. So was Joe Barbera, who also was a hell of a good sketch artist.

JBK: During the time you were with Disney, up until you left, did Ub Iwerks continue to do the title cards full time?

No. He still did the titles, but it wasn't a full-time job. Actually, one of the best things about animated cartoons is you didn't have the spoken titles in them. The balloons, yes, you still had those. But you can look at a comic strip and you don't have to read the balloons, you practically know what [has to be there]. So there were very few card titles. The only time we ever used them, we'd make a gag out of them. Like we'd say, "The morning broke," on a black card, and then it would shatter and there would be a sunrise. We'd use gags like that occasionally. [Also,] if it was night and then went to daytime, you'd use titles to denote the passage of time, or a change of scenery if it were necessary to explain it. So we

____

25 Allen became a director when the MGM cartoon department was reorganized in 1937, and continued to direct MGM cartoons (sometimes without credit) well into the 1940s.

used very few card titles. We used the balloons if they were necessary.[26]

Leon [Schlesinger] made main titles [in the 1920s] and that's what I did for him a couple of times: animation for main titles. For a picture, you had to have a main title, and a lot of those in those days would be done with animation. But we never used them, and by that time Ub had been in animation almost completely. He left Walt about the same time we did, but he went back. He made Flip the Frog, but he wasn't successful with it, and [in 1940] he went back to work for Walt.

[The machine is shut off, then started again for one more story.]

When Walt came out to California, the studio as such was still set up, he just left everything there. But we did see him off on the Sunset Limited. We went down to Union Station with the old Universal and tripod, to shoot him as the train went off into the distance. That was regular 35mm film.

Missakian, who married Nadine Simpson, did portrait photography. He had shot portraits of Walt, [back there in Kansas City]. Then [two years later], he, Nadine, and Maxwell came down to see us off to California, and we got out on the rear platform, too. Missakian got down there early so he could take pictures of us waving goodbye. But the train started before we knew it! [Laughs] So he had to run after the train, and we had to grab the camera from the back rail. We damn near lost the camera then. By that time we owned it, and we brought it out with us. But I'll never forget that. The poor guy! Because, you know, those tripods and cameras then were pretty heavy. But boy, he made it! And he got some pictures. We thought we had plenty of time before the train took off. Fortunately they don't start too fast. That was another story about that old camera. [Laughs]

© 2004 J.B. Kaufman

---

26 Ising's assertion is largely true—dialogue in Disney silents was delivered in balloons far more often than in titles—and his larger point, that animation is primarily a visual medium and dialogue is extraneous anyway, is also well taken. In fact, however, the Disney silents did employ a mix of balloons and title cards (as did other contemporary cartoons, including the Felix the Cat and Out of the Inkwell series). In the Alice Comedies, title cards were sometimes used to mask awkward exchanges between live and animated characters. In *Alice's Egg Plant* (1925), for example, a dialogue title appears in a scene in which the animated Julius hands a sheet of paper to the live-action Alice (Dawn O'Day). Julius is seen holding the page, which is simply drawn in his hand—cut to the title card—cut back to the scene, with Alice holding what is now a real sheet of paper. Audiences, then and now, usually fail to notice this modest sleight of hand.

David Hand (1900–1986)

Interviewed by Michael Barrier on November 21, 1973

David Hand was an immensely important figure at the Disney studio, but he was rarely interviewed, and his autobiography[1] says very little about his Disney career. Michael Barrier's interview with him—supplemented later by correspondence and phone interviews—was almost certainly the only time he talked extensively about his Disney experience for publication. In 1988, Mike permitted Frank Thomas and Ollie Johnston to read this transcript when they were writing their book on *Bambi*[2], and Thomas said that one part of the transcript, included here, was "the best description of Walt and the studio and the working arrangements I have ever read."

David Dodd Hand was born in New Jersey on January 23, 1900. Exactly thirty years later, he went to work for Walt Disney as an animator. Hand had at first pointed himself toward newspaper cartooning. He moved to Chicago to attend commercial art classes; then, when he ran out of money, he found a job at Wallace Carlson's Andy Gump studio. From there, he worked his way through the animated cartoon studios of New York City before taking a job at Disney's. He seems not to have distinguished himself in any of those earlier jobs, or even to have ingratiated himself with many of his fellow animators. At the Bray studio in New York, his colleague James Culhane later wrote, Hand "had an air of superiority that was foreign to the free and easy atmosphere."

Hand was not held in much higher esteem when he was animating at Disney's. His animation was "too mechanical," said Dick Lundy, another Disney animator in the early thirties. "He used to get a lot of birds, and he would chart the stuff out"—that is, Hand planned the flight of the birds in advance, as opposed to letting his animation flow. Such military precision, evident in Hand's animation of a flock of birds in *Flowers and Trees* (1932), has nothing to do with the way birds really fly.

Like his fellow director Burt Gillett—and Walt Disney himself—Hand probably lacked the ability to do anything particularly well, except be a boss. Unlike Gillett, though, Hand knew how to be a boss without challenging Disney's own authority.

---

1 David Hand, *Memoirs* (Martha Hand, 1986).

2 Frank Thomas and Ollie Johnston, *Bambi: The Story and the Film* (Stewart, Tabori and Chang, 1990).

Disney made Hand a director in 1933—his first cartoon was *Building a Building*, with Mickey and Minnie Mouse—and over the next few years Hand directed some of the best Disney shorts, among them *The Flying Mouse* (1934), *Who Killed Cock Robin?* (1935), and *Three Orphan Kittens* (1935). When Disney decided not to direct *Snow White and the Seven Dwarfs* himself, Hand got the assignment. Over the next few years, he served repeatedly as Disney's surrogate, overseeing the shorts and then *Bambi*, and exercising broad authority over many of the studio's operations. In all of these jobs, his manner was that of a very forceful, broad-stroke business executive.

Hand didn't linger over the details of each cartoon, as Wilfred Jackson did. Instead, he put a lot of work into assembling strong casts of animators for the shorts he directed. It wasn't special treatment from Walt Disney that permitted him to assemble his strong crews and schedule their work smoothly; he simply sought those advantages more aggressively than Jackson or Sharpsteen did. (His greater efficiency probably won him assignments that would otherwise have gone to one of his colleagues: the story outlines for both *The Flying Mouse* and *Who Killed Cock Robin?* show Jackson as the anticipated director.)

Hand became the quintessential Disney director—and the logical choice as Disney's second in command—because he devoted so much effort to giving his animators the characters and sequences that they could make the most of. Increasingly, in the thirties, a Disney director's job was to support and cushion his animators, with responsibilities of other kinds shifted elsewhere. When Hand spoke to one of Don Graham's classes early in 1936, he said the voices for the cartoons soon might be chosen, and the dialogue recorded, by the story department, before the story got to the director. "It would be fine for the director," he said, "because then he could give the animator more time." Walt Disney distributed the transcript of Hand's talk, with a laudatory cover memo, to the other directors, the story men, and the principal animators.

Jack Cutting, who worked briefly as Hand's assistant director in the mid-thirties, recalled that "the more he found you could do, he would unload it on you." But Hand was by no means a lazy man who dumped too much work on assistants. Instead, Cutting said, he was "ambitious, doing a lot of work...a hard driver"—delegating work to capable subordinates as a successful businessman might, that is, rather than sloughing it off.

"Walt was always in charge," said Eric Larson, who animated the owl for *Bambi*, "but Dave was a good wrangler." Wilfred Jackson "was the better director by quite a bit," the animator Frank Thomas said, "but Dave was the better organizer and driver." Chuck Couch, a writer on the

Disney shorts when Hand supervised them, remembered Hand as "a very practical guy.... If Dave liked something he'd tell you it was goddamn good. If it was bad he'd say it stinks. You always knew where you stood."

Hand's business-like attitudes came through in what Dick Lundy remembered as his advice when Lundy became a director in the late thirties: "Now, there's one thing you've got to do, Dick, you've got to make decisions and you've got to make them fast. If you're right 51 percent of the time, you're *right*."

In 1938, just after *Snow White*'s release, Hand drew up an elaborate organization manual. That manual was a response to the nightmarish logistical problems that arose during work on *Snow White*, when the studio grew rapidly and the old informal structures proved inadequate. It seems doubtful, though, that Hand's highly bureaucratic manual could ever have been the solution to such problems, even if Walt Disney had cooperated—as he clearly did not. Disney, like many another entrepreneur, bridled at the thought of submitting himself to the authority of an organization chart.

Hand's position was fundamentally untenable—he was second-in-command in an organization whose leader, younger than Hand himself, had no intention of ever stepping aside or sharing real power—and he finally left the studio in 1944. He spent several years in England, trying unsuccessfully to establish a Disney-level cartoon studio for the J. Arthur Rank organization, before returning to the United States and an uneventful career with the Alexander Film Company, which made commercials and industrial films in Colorado. In 1967, he moved to the small town of Cambria, on the California coast. He died there in 1986.

Michael Barrier interviewed Hand in Cambria on November 21, 1973; they met one evening at the town's Veterans Hall, when Mike and his wife were driving down the coast from San Francisco to Los Angeles. Hand was no longer the handsome young go-getter whose tailored sports coats led some Disney writers to nickname him "Shoulders", but he still had the direct, almost brusque manner of a businessman with important things to do. Predictably, he had little to say about the people who had worked under him; his attention was always on Walt Disney, and he was concerned most with reading his boss' moods and wishes.

David Hand: I was there, and I saw it, and I saw one man—who was a genius, no question about it—get the credit. It didn't bother me at the time, nor did it bother anyone else, because we were so busy, so immersed in developing this great art, and having someone—Walt—allow us to take the time to develop. Up to that time—and I had worked ten or eleven years before then—you couldn't have time to develop anything. You were given so much money, and you got the picture out for that amount, or you got out. It was a question of who got out first. With Walt, all the artists—and I include the story man, the contributor of ideas, the music composers, too—we were all so immersed in the development of this great art that we didn't want any publicity. In fact, we wouldn't talk, we didn't have time to talk. But further than that, I know, as it went on, that there was a prohibition from the front office: don't mention anybody but that one person, Walt. And if I'd set back and had time to meditate, I just hadn't liked it, because there was a tremendous creative contribution from these very fine artists. Without them, Walt didn't have a tool to work with.

But I must say he kept his tools sharp, and more credit to him. I wouldn't have been anything, and all these key men that you know about wouldn't have been anything in an animation studio without Walt. Walt fought the front office because they wanted him to make the cartoon for a price. I've heard him. I was with him enough to know that he practically threw Roy out of his office two or three times because Roy wanted him to make the pictures for a price in keeping with the market returns. But the costs of pictures increased each year. Roy would come in to the production department and say, "Walt, we can't spend so much, we're not going to be able to get the money back." And Walt, in his sharp, peculiar way, would say (Walt was younger than Roy, but he was the boss), he'd say, "Roy, *we'll* make the pictures, *you* get the money. Now goodbye, I'm busy." Then Roy would come to us, two or three of us together, and say, "Fellows, what are we going to do? You've got to work on Walt to spend less money on each picture!" Well, you couldn't work on Walt. That's the last thing you could do, work on Walt. Roy says, "I can't do anything with him. What are we going to do about it? I can't get the money." We didn't hear him.

Getting back to the artists—it was basically the opportunity that Walt gave all of us to do what we'd like, in line with what he thought was right. Walt couldn't really draw. I've seen him try, it was pathetic. Well, he didn't have to draw, did he? Better he didn't, because he would ask us animators, at the time I'm speaking of, to do things that were impossible to do. But *he* didn't know it. Good thing he wasn't an animator. As a director, when I had been an animator, I had to be considerate of the animator, and not ask him to do things that were impossible. That was my weakness, Walt's strength.

I started [at the Disney studio], I believe, two days after Ub Iwerks left. I started on my birthday, and how could I miss it. Ub had quit the Friday before, according to my understanding, which I wouldn't argue about. So I was that close behind Ub; I knew Ub later, but not at the studio. Walt talked about Ub to me. He said he was terrible when it came to staying at the drawing board. "His car was parked outside in the driveway"—very small place—he said. "Ub was out there all day working on his car, fixing it up, putting new things on it. I said, 'Ub, you can get a mechanic to do that job for ten dollars, come back in here and animate.'" They didn't get along, as you know, and Ub, of course, eventually went back to Disney as a technician [in 1940]. That was his forte, although he was a wonderful artist.

The other peculiar thing is, Walt said to us—there were probably eight or ten of us at the time, and Ub had just left—he said, "You fellows can have Ub's share of the business." I thought that was very nice. Of course, it was only a little studio, and no one had visualized the eventual size of it, so a few dollars more a week, or a year, what did it matter? But that's the last time Walt ever mentioned it. I often wondered, as time went on, what happened to it. I suspect his brother got after him and said, "You crazy idiot!"

Michael Barrier: You didn't take him up on the offer right away?

Oh, he felt badly that Ub left. You know the background of the two of them. From where I sit, Ub was the man who put Disney in the animation field professionally because he was a professional animator, he could draw the characters, and Walt couldn't do any of that as well as Ub, so I think Ub had a lot to do with it.

Anyway, when I went there, we had had a little bull's-eye Moviola; you might have seen them. Not the Moviolas that project onto a little screen; it was just a magnification bull's-eye. And Walt would cock his eye—we would make our animation and have it photographed in pencil [the pencil drawings would be photographed for test purposes before they were traced in ink onto celluloid] and put into a loop—and Walt would get his frown, one eye poked into that bull's-eye, and he was looking at it with his foot on the pedal, and he'd start shaking his head, and he'd start really tearing an animator apart, if he didn't get what he thought the animator should get. I can remember an instance of some animation I did when I was first there. We were not using assistants to any extent in those days; the animator usually did every drawing, and he did it cleaned up. We didn't always have an assistant to put the in-between drawings in, which is the accepted system today. We made extremes, and in-betweened them ourselves much of the time.

MB: Dave Smith [the Disney studio's archivist] has written that one reason Ub and Walt quarreled was that Walt wanted Ub to use an in-betweener.

I don't know about that, but it sounds like Ub. It seems to me it was a transitional period—sometimes we used in-betweeners, and at other times, when there was a difficult bit to do, we did our own in-betweening.

Anyway, the animator had to get his drawings completed, and they were not rough drawings, at that time they were cleaned-up drawings, every one of them. Then he had them photographed. The test film was delivered to him for viewing. Well, that's a lot of time wrapped up in those drawings. I'm only going to make a point by saying that I well remember at this time that I had a particular Mickey Mouse taxicab scene to do [for *Traffic Troubles*, 1931], and I did my very best with it—as I of course would—and got it on the Moviola with Walt, and he squinted and squirmed and grunted, and said, no, it didn't have enough exaggerated action to it. I said OK, and back I went to my desk. Five times I brought that corrected scene to him, and each time I made it more exaggerated, and each time he turned it down. I thought, "What does this crazy man want?" I'd been in the business eleven years then, and Walt had much less time in the business—I never thought of that, though, I never thought that he didn't know as much as I, I never thought that, I just thought that he ought to know that this animation of mine is acceptable, that was all. So, the fifth time I went back to my desk, and again, making all the in-betweens, and the drawings cleaned up nicely, and had it tested—I went back this time, happy that at last Walt would approve it. He looked at it, shook his head, and walked away. I was broken up! It wasn't right that I should have to do it that often.

Finally, I thought, "I'm going to show Walt he can't be that smart with me"—I'm a year older than him, and even though that didn't matter, it was just that he wasn't an older man—I said to myself, "I'm going to show that fellow a trick or two." So [I] went back to my desk to redo this scene a sixth time, and I said, "I'm going to make this thing so extreme, so outlandish, so crazy, that he'll say, "Well, Dave, I didn't mean to exaggerate it *that* much." So I did, I was really dirty—the only time I remember being dirty with Walt—and I made that thing so outlandish, and so extreme, I was ashamed of what I had done. But I brought the new test in very self-righteously and put it on for Walt, and said, "All right, Walt, I did this thing over again, I hope it's OK," while slyly watching for him to explode—fly off the handle. He put his foot on the pedal, and he started the loop around and around and around, looking at it and looking at it. Then he stopped the loop and looked up at me with a big smile and said, "There! You've got it! Why didn't you do it that way in the first place?"

That lesson stuck with me as I progressed through the studio, into supervising animator and then director. A supervising animator had three or four juniors, and he would take a small section of the picture, or a third of the picture, from the director and farm it out to his juniors, and he would work with them to show them how to get what he was supposed to be able to get. That was a part of the development of the animator in the studio in the early days, and continued, juniors working under seniors, and seniors being responsible for juniors. The lazier the senior was, the more the junior got to do because the senior would sit and read books and make the junior do the job properly, and that's how the junior learned so well.

So that lesson about exaggeration stayed with me through the supervising animation to the direction, and the supervising director that I eventually became. I never forgot that, and I think it might have shown up a little bit in my working with Walt—what he wanted, I suppose I could convey to an animator.

MB: Where had you worked before you came to Disney's?

I worked with J. R. Bray. Milt Gross was making a series, for Bray, *Nize Baby.* Later, I worked with Walt Lantz. When sound came in, it was obvious to anyone in the business that this was something helpful to the cartoon medium—but how to use it? How to get the sound effects and voices to sync with the animation? I believe that all the studios at this time began trying to unlock the secret. I know that I was trying desperately to figure it out, and couldn't. And no one else seemed able to do it. At this time, all the big studios were located in New York—that was the place where the action was. Disney was in Los Angeles, but he didn't count, really. Well, all of a sudden a cartoon was showing on Broadway—with sound, and perfectly [synchronized]. It set the animation world on fire. *Steamboat Willie.* Not only did it wake up the animation business, it became the rave of the movie houses. People talked about it, and sent their friends to see it. And Walt Disney was on his way!

I think I know the man who conceived it—Wilfred Jackson. I believe Willie knew the mechanics of music, as I did, too, but I didn't have his mechanical know-how. He knew—as anybody should have known— that twenty-four frames make a second, and you make twenty-four drawings, and jump them up and down in a second, and it's in beat, in rhythm, and so on. That, of course, gave Walt the jump on everybody. Walt's studio was no better—not as good, really—in animation as other studios. But Walt got the jump on all the other studios because he had synchronization. That was only the beginning. Walt had genius, too, but without first getting that jump on the other studios, nobody would listen to a genius.

When he synchronized the cartoon with the sound—music and so forth—it was like a whole new world opening up. [For me,] who had been in the business so long, to see these characters synchronized with sound, it was fantastic! I rather thought that that's something I ought to be able to do, but I couldn't, so I had to go out to Walt Disney. It was so simple when I learned how; it wasn't long before the other studios unlocked the secret, too. The way I see it, it gave Walt the edge on the other studios, then he had the good sense to make an animator do a thing right. He also had two more things: he had intuitive judgment, and he never forgot a gag he ever heard. I'm not kidding you. He never admitted a gag wasn't original with him, but you could many times trace the source of them. I don't know that he even knew it himself. I've sat in story meetings with Walt, and heard someone—A, B, or C—bring up a spontaneous gag, to go in a certain place. Walt's sitting there frowning. Looking usually someplace else, and before the meeting is over, he gets the idea out of the air—excitedly explains it—and it goes in the picture. He never even heard it mentioned earlier, except that he *did* hear it. What did he have, a catalog of thought that stuck it all away and then flipped it out? I don't know what it was, but I know he thought it came spontaneously from him. And it was with all his ideas. I call it genius; of course I call it genius, I'm not running the man down. He also knew how to get it on the screen.

Another interesting thing—I used to, as a director, fight with the story department—and Walt was one of them—because I didn't think an idea was funny; and a director had the final responsibility for the results of a picture. Once he took it into his room, it was his baby; no excuses. So I would fight with them. Walt was in there, too. They would fight back, and I would argue, and finally we would revise the idea so that I would be happy with it. Then I had to go through the same thing with the animator. He didn't have to take a scene that he didn't think was right, so he and I would sit in the director's room, and we would argue and fight—not to get him to take that scene if he didn't like it, but to try to get to work around until it was *his* scene, and then he could produce it on the screen. So it was with the director; when it became his picture, he could produce it, provided he was a good enough director. There would be ideas that I didn't like, and I would say I didn't like them. And the story men would work on them, and change them around until I was half-happy with them. Once there was one idea I just thought was rather terrible, and I said so, and Walt fought me, and he got mad at me; and he could be rather unreasonable, at times. Of course, he was the boss, but he usually was very understanding. But not this time. So I took the idea—I didn't want to—and went into the director's room with it. Some time later Walt came in, and I said, "Walt, I still don't like it." He said, "Oh, it's a good one, Dave, you do it. Do it just the way we told it to you." So I did; believe me, I did. I worked hard to sell it to the animator, and he didn't help. They'd just sit there and [say] "Yeah, yeah." Sometimes, they wouldn't know whether it was good or bad. The scene came out on the screen—we always had our previews, sneak previews—and the darned gag fell flat as a pancake. The next day—there was always a post-mortem—I said, "Walt, I didn't ever think that gag was any good." He said, "Jeez, Dave, you just didn't do it right." So I mumbled to myself and thought, "You can't win with Walt."

[The episode in question involved a scene in *The Flying Mouse* (1934). Hand described what happened in a letter to Barrier in May 1975: "The mouse was being blown backward through the air, out of control. He was a sympathetic character in a sad plight. The 'laugh' gag was that his rear end would make a 'bull's eye' into a large thorn sticking out of a rosebush stem. Now, for me, the idea itself was not funny—especially happening to a pathetic little flying mouse. But I had been previously overruled in story, so when the picture got to me, I decided to play the impaling idea down as much as possible. However, Walt caught up with me when I was getting it ready for the animator. We had more argument, and I lost. Walt insisted that I make the thorn long, dark, and sharp—and that the mouse's rear end get buried clear up to the hilt. And further to this, that I have the music build up to a 'screech' accent. That poor mouse! The audience did not laugh at it, but it was one of the many instances where I found Walt to be surprisingly sadistic. He seemed to enjoy 'hurt' gags more than a lot of people."]

The development of the animators really took place with Walt's encouragement—insistence, actually. The good animator, as soon as he became any kind of a top quality animator, got burdened with kids who didn't know much about animation. It might be Fred Moore I'm talking about, but at the time Freddy Moore came in, he didn't know anything, and he went in as a junior, and the senior animator was burdened with him. He'd give him run-throughs, and jumps, and bits of this and bits of that. Of course, the sharp boys soon learned how to animate properly, and they had that feeling of "Disney". We were all "Disney", we never went against Walt Disney, we had married him, we wanted to do what he wanted—not necessarily because he was a boss so much as he was a leader, and the stuff was going out in the theaters, and people were liking it. So, throughout the years, besides all the details of animation development that we had in the studio—special classes and such—the basic system was the key animator taking on juniors, till they became, themselves, toward key. We had, to my way of reasoning as a director, three grades of animators: the key animator, the junior animator, and the assistant to the junior. Key animators were cast as you cast a character actor. Some of them could do one kind of thing, and some another; one kind of thing not so well as the other. They became specialists in some kinds of animation. So we cast them, and the juniors under them were learning that kind of animation, or else they would be moved to somebody else if they showed greater talent in another kind of animation. So a key animator ended up with rather a fair group of assistants in one manner or another, all developing, and all under the pressure of quality, and Disney in back of it.

MB: In many cartoon directors' films, you can see in the animators' work the director's personality, and what he wanted.

That would be true—I think you mentioned someone like Chuck Jones [at Warner Bros.], and his strong poses—but in the Disney studio, that was Walt.

MB: But, even so, you had to get the animators to do what Walt wanted.

Yes, and they wanted to do what Walt wanted, too, there was no problem there. They worked hard to do it.

MB: You've mentioned that you never saw any politics, that the competition among directors for animators was friendly.

Yes, that is right, and I would have seen politics being played because I was close in animation, close in direction and over-all studio supervision. I never had anyone come to me playing what we termed politics. I think a large part of the lack of it was that Walt didn't encourage political maneuvering, and he did not like apple polishing. I'm not a politician; but some people are naturally bent that way, and I think that Walt would sense it, squint and frown, and turn and walk away. That's why we weren't bothered with it in the studio.

The animator himself became like one you would cast for normal [live-action] pictures. He became a certain type of person who could do certain kinds of animation better—not that he couldn't animate almost anything, but he did certain things better than anyone else in the studio could. He was naturally cast on specific types of characters and business. He would take with him his juniors and then give them the kinds of things that they seemed to like best.

MB: Were there ever cases of animators who were best at a certain kind of animation, but who really wanted to do some other kind? I've heard that Milt Kahl, for example, would really prefer to do wilder, more cartoony animation, instead of the realistic animation that he does.

I'm smiling because certain animators were problems. They wanted to do one kind of thing, they couldn't do it well, but they insisted they could do it. I always thought of an animator as a highly creative artist who had a world of his own turning around inside him. An animator, particularly, couldn't see anywhere beyond himself. There were some animators who did insist that they could do other work better, and did get a chance at it, and either [did] it or fail[ed] at it. We would probably give it to them to quiet them, as it were. Any particular instance that you might mention would be rather general in the studio, with a lot of animators, who are very temperamental. Oh, man, working with a studio full of artists, you've got yourself a problem. They all had temperaments of one kind or another, or they wouldn't be artists, and the better ones had more temperament—not all of them, but some of them. So, that would be true, but wouldn't it be silly for a studio, and Walt in particular, to say to Joe, or Jack, or whomever, "No, you just do what you're told and stay where you are?" A top man? A top man you work with, you don't want to misdirect him in any manner.

MB: Speaking of the different animators' styles, the Disney cartoons seem to have succeeded better than those of other studios in keeping a consistency of style throughout the cartoon. If it's possible to get specific, how would the director do that, working with the animators?

Well, to begin, he would object to the casting of an animator on his picture, if the type of work was entirely out of his character. When a picture would be cast, in the shorts, the director would sit with Walt and the production manager, who knew where everybody was and when they were coming off their present assignment—a terribly complicated thing in a big studio. The director would have to know the animators, and he did know them because he grew up with them. He would say, "I would like to have A, B, C, and D." "Well, you can't have B, because he still has a problem on the other picture, and they've got to do a lot of that stuff over." "Well, how about L or M? They do work like that." I'd give them a little less of the important stuff. So there was a sort of working back and forth until you got a crew that could pretty much handle the kind of picture that you were working on. And there were different types of pictures. Now, these [other cartoon] studios you speak of, I don't think they cared about that as much.

MB: Most studios would have a crew of animators that would work with the same director, year in and year out. It sounds as if at Disney's, they would shift around.

Yes, we didn't have that at Disney. We'd cast the man for the kind of thing he could do on the kind of picture. We had a great many productions going through, as you know. The most interesting thing is the organizing of that vast amount of talent.

MB: I recently re-read the Robert Field book, *The Art of Walt Disney* [published in 1942; not to be confused with the 1973 book of the same title, by Christopher Finch], which deals in large part with the organization of the studio. From the book, it sounds as if the studio was very well organized, and yet also very loose, so people could be shifted around as they were needed.

I had a lot to do with that, in organizing the studio, because I was eventually in that particular capacity, where Walt was in the story department and I was taking care of the rest of the details of production. There was so much manpower, and each one of them was a temperament that you just couldn't push around like you push "nuts and bolts" people around. The problem was to get a group of people to the right place at the right time, in order that they would be able to handle the kind of work that was coming through. The *kind* of work—not any work, the kind of work that was coming through. So it took a vast organization of controls, and memos that went out continuously. That's hard enough in a big studio; but we had a boss-man who didn't care anything about army organization. He didn't care about the general being the top man, and that he should go through the brigadier in giving orders, and on down the line to the private. He thought he could, and he did, tell the corporal to have the captains and the majors see that the rest of the privates were over here doing something else. And if you were a corporal in that studio, you hopped when the general told you to.

I'm talking about Walt, of course. Walt didn't care anything about the details of organization. And he caused a great deal of trouble by ordering a certain man, or his group of men, to do something else *right now*. This whole organization was supposedly working properly, and we were so interrelated, all of us, that when this happened we would immediately tell the other guys what went on, so it didn't go on for long, probably half an hour, before the man that Walt had told to change something, some routine, saw to it that the information got right back up to me.

Then, right away, my secretary had to start those memos going out, changing the order of things. We never tried to deny Walt the right to do it, but we had to get the memos out to all the other departments saying that signals had been changed, and we're going to do it this other way. Then the organizational charts we had, telling how the operation was to take place, had to be changed—it was a mess.

Of course, the kind of man Walt was, you couldn't expect him to care anything about organization, and he didn't. And he would do these things, and it didn't matter who he spoke with; but fortunately, we had a vast Dictaphone system, we could call anyone with a button, never mind going through operators. This was before we went over to Burbank, this was on Hyperion. The director had about thirty keys he could push, to get anybody he wanted, and the animators had certain keys they could push—not as big a set of them. So it wasn't long before everybody in the studio who was concerned knew the signals had been changed. And that's how the studio was run. Except in the meantime, we tried to have organization. I could go on for hours about organization, but that's about the way it was. It was a very strict organization; there was an organizational setup, and it took an awful lot of time and a lot of people to see that it worked.

MB: Did this degree of organization become necessary when you began work on the features?

It developed during the first feature, and we couldn't have produced the feature without it. I'm speaking of *Snow White*, which I was cast on as supervising director. We had a deadline, and there was also a very definite financial problem at the studio at the time, and we almost went broke. We had two deadlines: one was to get a rough viewing product ready for the bankers, an example picture—some pencil animation, some stills, some music, whatever—to get some more money from the bankers. We then had spent $750,000 (all Disney money, I believe), which was a lot of money in those days, and we needed nearly another $750,000 to finish it. So that was the first deadline, to get the preliminary picture ready so we could get $750,000 more. They did give us $750,000 to finish *Snow White*, which made a total cost of about $1.5 million [officially, the negative cost was $1,488,422.74]. Then we had the deadline to completely finish it before Christmas, for Christmas preview. Everybody worked very hard to get that picture out, and did get it out, on deadline. But we couldn't have done it without organization, we just couldn't handle a thing like that without organization.

MB: The studio's employment expanded tremendously, didn't it, when you began work on *Snow White*? I imagine that would have been chaotic without organization, adding all those people.

That's a story in itself, too, the adding of the people and the training and developing of them. There was no place to get them, but out on the open market. There was one fortunate thing, of course; that was done during the Depression, and good artists needed work. It made a difference. In other words, we were on the buying end, and the artist only had himself to sell, and he needed a job. I think that was one of the reasons we were able to get so many good people at that time. I know that we had 1,150 artists when we finished *Snow White* [actually, the studio's employment didn't reach that level until work was under way on later features like *Pinocchio* and *Bambi*]. The cost of pictures when I went there, I think was about thirty-five hundred dollars for Mickey Mouse. They went up to five thousand dollars, and that's when Roy started fussing with Walt because he couldn't get five thousand dollars for a picture. You do know that the distributors were giving pictures away before Walt came along, don't you? Walt didn't like Roy complaining about costs, and he told Roy that he was going to make the pictures better. They got up to five thousand dollars and Roy felt terrible about that because he had to go out and find five thousand dollars for every picture.

To cut a long story short, they got up to fifteen thousand dollars—$16,500 was one, I think, and that was too much. They couldn't, at that time, get that much money out of the market. That's how the feature idea was born. Walt said, "If we are making twenty pictures at 650 feet, and we are getting fifteen thousand dollars for one picture of 650 feet, why don't we make ten pictures for $150,000 and call it a feature?" So far as I know, it was Walt's idea to make the feature; I don't know how much he talked it over with other people. But the reasoning was—I know that because of the discussions—well, look, they're only paying us so much, and we can't get any more out of the market, so [if] we stick ten of them together, then we can get maybe three or four hundred thousand dollars, whereas now they're only paying us $150,000, with no profit. Well, you know *Snow White* grossed I think it was ten million, which was exceptional at that time. Good reasoning. All the key animators went on the feature, of course, and the other guys stayed on the shorts, and the shorts suffered because of it, and never did quite recover.

I asked him [Walt] to please let the animators invest in the company, and his answer was (and his thinking is interesting because now Disney is public), "No, Dave. Do you think I'm going to let an animator invest in this company and get a certain amount of investment, and get out of the studio and sit on his ass and let these other fellows staying behind do all the work while he doesn't contribute anything? I'll never allow that." And he wouldn't allow us to invest in his studio because of it. That, of course, upset me terribly because the men were so dedicated, that he should not let them have some stock; but he wouldn't.

MB: *Snow White* is roughly the length of ten or eleven shorts, and yet its cost was much, much more than ten times the cost of a short. What led to the great increase in costs?

Very simple. I'm being facetious when I say there were seven dwarfs, but it's true. More than that, Disney was insisting on a quality—and also he got mixed up in the multiplane camera, which was very expensive— he was insisting upon a quality where it was tremendously costly; and besides this, the animator didn't have a Donald Duck or a Mickey Mouse to animate, he had dimensional characters. A marvelous accomplishment, but every key animator of any note had to draw every character, not in graphic form, but in personality. When you can make the characters live the way the dwarfs lived, and get every animator to do it, and make that same character look alike, and act alike, you've done something—and that costs money.

MB: They couldn't rely on formulas....

Well, when you say "formulas", I know you don't mean a circle for a head or a pear-shaped body, you mean a formulized character, the characteristics in the character. We used to sit as a group, in the large sound stage we had at that time, and people would get up and act out their impression of a particular character. The most interesting thing to me in the whole studio is something that's quite hidden, to make a character come alive, be born. Come to life dimensionally, not the way some of it's done. Every key animator had to know that character, and it was a great deal of effort to get every animator to know the character completely. I don't know if you appreciate the amount of creative effort that comes out of an animator to make the character live a certain way. Not Mickey Mouse, Donald Duck, and Pluto; they had few subtle shades. These *Snow White* characters that actually have these little idiosyncrasies, little twists and turns and little walks. Every animator had to know how to do it. And there were, still, seven dwarfs, and, of course, the live-action [that is, based on live-action film] Snow White and the Prince and such, and also the beautiful backgrounds, and the designs of the dwarfs' house, and the interiors, and so forth, which was mostly [Albert] Hurter's stuff. Tremendous cost to that.

MB: How much animation had to be done over because of this? Was there a great deal of re-animating?

There always has been in the Disney studio. There always was while I was there, and if the animator learned from it—I did—it was well worth the effort. What you should have asked was, how much was thrown out of the picture?

MB: There were two complete sequences thrown out, weren't there?

Very costly and finished at that, in animation.

MB: Weren't they building a bed in one sequence, and eating soup in the other? What was the reason for not using those sequences?

They didn't seem necessary to the direct storyline that we were following. You know, at the Disney studio—at least when I was there, I don't know about now—the storyline was the most important part of a production. There was no hit or miss; it was all very hard work in the story department. Consequently, when these sequences were in, and the footage was so much, and it's too costly to finish, and it proved not to be really directly concerned with the picture—that was it.

We wore the sweatbox out—we called it a sweatbox, you undoubtedly know why [because of the nervousness the animators felt when Disney was looking at their animation], and later a small projection room probably half the size of this [the small room where the interview took place]; and they were quite posh. The seats, and the screen, and the projectionist up back, and a place for the secretary and such. It was well organized. I would say, only at a guess, a quarter of the things, a third of the things, had to be done over. Not all done over, but scenes. I don't know that any important scene was ever passed without some work on it. I don't know that any animator ever presented a scene to a director—I'm talking about *Snow White* now—that didn't have some corrections. And if the director couldn't find them, when Walt saw a sequence he would find them, and all the things to be done over. That's how good pictures are made.

MB: What would be the nature of these corrections?

Almost anything. Grumpy wasn't grumpy enough—his actions didn't fit the force of the dialogue. The pre-scored [that is, recorded in advance of the animation] dialogue was shouting and forceful, but Grumpy just didn't seem to be portraying in his expressions and actions that piece of dialogue. Or it might be the dwarfs' dance, where they're all dancing around with Snow White. They weren't happy enough, they weren't bouncy enough, they weren't expressing the feeling of the music. Things like that. Or when Dopey got up on Sneezy's shoulders and danced around with Snow White, he wasn't silly enough. These corrections go way beyond the simple mechanics of animation. The best animators, of course, would have to do things over, which was no stigma to them.

MB: Would you ever have cases when the layouts and the animation weren't working the way you'd planned? Say the lines of action were conflicting—would you ever have to go back one step and rework the layouts as well?

That would be rare. The reason is that the layout man sat in the room with the director. The director had a large desk area, and the layout man had his own little corner—large rooms, they were. We called them "music rooms", but they were directors' rooms. The director and the layout man would go over this sequence—three or four or five times—and the director would very carefully explain to the layout man exactly what took place, and when it took place—"when", relative to the other actions of the scene—where he entered, how he entered, what he did—climb a tree or fall in a hole, whatever, and over here, maybe, and over there— and the layout man would then make, promptly, a rough sketch with many positions where the character would be in the scene, just rough. The layout man knew the characters pretty well to draw them, not to animate them. So the layout man would—to the best of his understanding of what the scene was about—make two or three rough sketches and present them to the director, who was sitting there, maybe busy for the minute, but nevertheless available, and the director would go over them with the layout man, and agree or disagree on what the layout man had done—whatever the perspective was, was the character shown going far enough away and coming up in the foreground enough, and all that kind of stuff, until the layout man got the director's OK and was prepared to go into his final layout drawings. When he went into those, he pretty much understood, and the director very much agreed, that that was what was wanted.

Now, there usually was not a change, but there could have been a change when the animator came in to pick up the scene. Because, as I explained to you earlier, the animator *had* to be satisfied. There was no business of telling him to do it or else. The director's job was to sell the animator, the animator not necessarily really knowing what was good or not in ideas. Nothing against the animator; he was not a story man, he was not an idea man, he was an animator. But sometimes something would stick in his craw and he wouldn't like it, so we'd have to work it over and get it so he *would* like it. Change the timing on the exposure sheets, change the layout, do anything to get that animator satisfied and happy, when he left the room. I think you'll agree, in talking with any of the animators at the Disney studio, that when they left the room they were satisfied that the scene would work. So when they got back on the desk, and did the scene, and presented the rough animation to the director, then the discussion took place: "But you didn't do it enough." They had to follow the exposure sheet; the animator even helped to change an exposure sheet, if he didn't agree with the director's timing, and he didn't necessarily agree—that is, the key animators. They knew what they were doing; they'd say, "I don't have time to do that." And a director would argue, but nevertheless, he would cut out some action so as to give the animator the time he felt he needed. So, when the animator left the room, the fact is that he agreed that he had a good scene. So now he's returned with the rough animation of the whole scene—and the director said, "But you didn't do it the way we agreed." There were never any big arguments. The director would then act it out in some manner, and the animator would go back and make his changes, or get his assistant to make them—it didn't matter. When he came back the next time, it might be right, or something else might require changing. Then it went through the normal routine of in-betweening all the drawings and cleaning up, and into the other departments.

MB: You mentioned timing—so an animator would say that there wasn't enough time allotted on the exposure sheet for him to make this particular action convincing?

Yes, an experienced animator would say that. The director had to time the whole picture, half-second by half-second, and he could of course always use a stopwatch—sometimes you would get a feel of a thing without a stopwatch for ten or fifteen seconds, but not very technical, close actions. He'd have to time those out. So there would be a discussion, and the animator would say, "Yeah, yeah, that's right, I didn't see it that way. Yes, I can do that." Or, "No, I can't do it." You'd certainly give him time to do it, or he would say, "Well, I can't do a scene like that. No wonder it doesn't come out, you wouldn't let me have the time!"

MB: You and the other Disney directors were all former animators yourselves, weren't you?

We had to be. Not in our studio was there ever a director who wasn't an animator. No, the animator wouldn't have looked up to you—he wouldn't have trusted you. And you had to be a key animator; you couldn't be a junior someplace, you had to know what you were talking about. Naturally. He had confidence in you. Well, that's only proper, isn't it? We had confidence in Walt, the animators had confidence in the directors, that they knew what they were talking about, especially if the director would discuss and argue with them and work with them, to get the thing the way the animator thought it ought to be, so he would do it properly.

MB: How did you become a director yourself?

The first direction I did was at Fleischer. How was it Walt picked me? I don't know. I don't know why the Fleischers picked me. I was an idea man, I always have been an idea man. Not necessarily the best idea man, but an idea man. I found myself writing and directing the *Out of the Inkwell* cartoons. From animation—which I did—to writing and directing. I must have had some executive ability, or I couldn't have handled the Disney operation, and I couldn't have later gone over to Rank. It must have been there, but I don't know how, except that the boss man must have recognized it. Why Walt ever picked me to direct *Snow White* when there were five other directors—I don't know. He told me that I shouldn't be in the business, on my first directorial job on shorts. That was *Building a Building*. Walt had the extra animators, and I suppose he saw a directorial ability in me—I say that humbly—so he gave me this story that was turned down by other directors and said that I was to direct it. This was my introduction to Disney direction, although I had directed before Disney. He didn't care about what I'd done before. But he wouldn't give me any of the key animators, the guys who could animate. He gave me these little, junior fellows. He said, "Hell, Dave, you've worked with juniors as supervising animator, you can work with these fellows." Well, there was a lot of personality stuff, and how do you get it out of juniors? Anyway, when the picture was previewed, I felt happy because I happened to have counted the number of laughs in the picture because it was my picture. Never mind the number, it was up there—actually, twenty-one. I was very happy—happy for the studio, not for myself. The next day, Walt came into my room, and he stayed through noon hour—about an hour and a half—and told me where I should have been, instead of in an animation studio, and how did I ever think I could direct. This is true: Walt isn't here to defend himself, but I assure you it was true. He knocked me down until I was lower than a snake's belly. I don't know why he did it, because I know the picture was all right: I heard the audience at the sneak preview. A very peculiar man, Walt was. But I took it. I took it, and before long I was directing *Snow White*. [Laughing] Don't ask me how I got it.

I must tell you, a very funny thing happened. We had a meeting on *Snow White*, on one of the sequences, and the director is always in on a sequence when it's finally getting ready to be delivered, and they had an action with one of the dwarfs moving around the room, and you had to work to a certain length—this was working to music, and had about thirty seconds for this particular action. Walt was a marvelous pantomimist, a marvelous actor. If you said it to him, he would grump and walk away, but he was. And, of course, when he would get one of his expressions on his face with an animator, you'd better get it on the screen, which you usually did. He had a rubber face, it seemed to me. Anyway, I couldn't see the action getting completed in the time allotted. I said—because we always deferred to Walt, never mind how many other people were in room, you worked with Walt, and talked to him, and told him it didn't work, you didn't tell somebody else—I said, "Walt, the animator can't do it in that time." He said [imitating Disney's grumpy voice], "Hell, yes, Dave, you can do it in that time." He got up and did it again—very good acting. I said, "Well, it looked too long to me, Walt." He didn't know it, but I had a stopwatch hidden in my pocket. A dirty trick. And I said to him, "Walt, do it once more for me, will you, please?" "Oh, sure." Now, it was supposed to be done in thirty seconds—not thirty-two seconds—and he'd get up, and he'd go all through it—marvelous stuff, you know. Lots of action in it, lots of things to be done. And he got all through and he said, "There! You see, there it is—thirty seconds." And I pulled this stopwatch out, which I had started with his acting. I should never have done it. I looked at my watch and I said, "That was *fifty-five* seconds, Walt." I learned a lesson. He didn't like that kind of thing, he didn't like that at all, no. He had an eyebrow that went up and helped to part his hair, and it went up, and the other one went down. He had a very disturbing frown. He didn't say a word. He just turned and stomped out of the room. He hadn't said anything. What was there to say?

He was a funny man. You didn't usually cross him. You didn't tell him he didn't know what he was talking about, ever. We knew better than that. But we did do things behind his back that he didn't want done, in order to get a job done.

MB: When you first came to the Disney studio, I guess in 1929 or 1930....

January 1930, the last of the month.

MB: You've already mentioned the synchronization of the sound, but what other things was Disney doing that struck you as different from what you'd been exposed to before?

The Moviola, the pencil tests. You saw a negative, you understand that; it was a negative delivered to you in a loop, for your scene. The scene might be four, five, six, eight, ten seconds. Your loop went around through that Moviola. The Moviola was set at twenty-four [frames] per second, although you could run it very slowly and back it up, back and forth, back and forth. That was the innovation, and that was the thing that allowed the animator—and allowed Walt—to see what the animator was going to put on the screen, so the animation didn't get all the way through production before he could see it.

MB: They were already making pencil tests when you went to work there?

Yes, I remember standing by the hour, looking at tests. Just one little bull's-eye, you know. The damned thing stood up so high, and you put your foot on the pedal; that's all they had.

MB: What really distinguished Disney from the New York studios was the striving for personality in the characters. Were you conscious of that when you came to Disney, was it already in evidence?

It was not in open evidence, but such a thing as what Walt was striving for grew within him and the animators—a unity of development, of a desire for the better, for the very best obtainable. Walt, of course, was the spirit in back of it all, when he could tell the front office, "You get the money, we'll make the pictures." You never heard that before, not in the cartoon business. It was always, "Yes, sir, we'll do it for thirty-five hundred dollars"—and you'd better.

MB: I've always heard the general statement that his story mind was what set him apart.

Yes, this is true. Well, that's part of what his genius was, [but] he had it more than there. He intuitively knew pretty much—didn't make many mistakes—what was right and what was wrong. Like a woman, who doesn't reason the way a normal executive would reason about something. He worked by intuition a lot.

MB: I've heard that he would come into a meeting, where say nineteen or twenty people were working on a problem, and he would suddenly reach out and pull the solution out of the air.

It wasn't quite that spontaneous. I would say that whether it was a good solution or not, if Walt decided it was, that was the end of the conference. That's fairly stated. So, I wouldn't say that was necessarily true. I've seen us all struggle by the hour, by the week, with Walt in the meetings, struggling over solutions. He didn't get them that easy. But he did have a good memory, which helped him, and also he used intuition.

He and I used to belong to a riding group out here in Santa Barbara, called the Rancheros Visitaderos, and every May they rode for a week up over the mountains and stopped at different ranches—all men, stag [according to records in the Disney Archives, those outings took place in the late thirties]. He would ride along with me—these were long rides, up from Santa Barbara over to the Santa Ynez Valley. He would talk at me, all the time, riding along, what we should do on some picture or problem, and how we should do it, and I got so full and so confused, with his changing his mind, that I eventually—the second or third day starting out—would hide out, behind the big oaks, with my horse, until he went on down the trail with some other Rancheros, then I'd go along merrily, to keep away from him. He was wearing me down; he didn't know anything else, he couldn't talk anything else but that studio. When [he was] at home, he'd go over to the studio about every night, you know, and look through animators' drawings….

Walt never praised; I don't ever remember him praising me or anybody else. I don't want to be unjust with the man, [but] I don't remember him ever saying, "Gee, you did a fine job," slapping you on the back. Never that. Never that. And he prohibited us from looking at other studios' pictures; I mean to study them, in the early days. We'd come in and say, "Oh, boy, we saw a lousy"—whatever picture. "Let's get a print to look at." Walt said, "Look, don't go looking at that kind of stuff. Just look at good stuff. If you find good stuff, let's look at it, but don't look at bad stuff." We were so happy to be so much better, but he took us down, he didn't care about that.

MB: So, if you didn't get criticized by Walt, that was your praise, more or less?

Well, yeah. The theater was our—and his, too—criterion. It was our answer. If it wasn't good, he didn't have to tell us. We knew it, you could tell it. I'm talking about the key men now. He didn't have to scold people. If any scolding was to be done it was in the sweatbox before the preview. At the time of the preview, the die was cast, and he stood responsible with everybody else for what was on the screen.

© 2004 Michael Barrier

Bill Tytla (1904–1968)

Interviewed by George Sherman on May 13, 1968

Frank Thomas and Ollie Johnston once wrote about Vladimir Tytla: "Bill was powerful, muscular, high-strung and sensitive, with a tremendous ego. Everything was "feelings" with him. Whatever he animated had the inner feelings of his characters expressed through very strong acting. He did not just get inside Stromboli, he *was* Stromboli and he lived the part." This new style of animation proved to be a revolution at the Disney Studio and earned Tytla his special status in the history of animation as one of the true geniuses of the medium.

Bill Tytla was born on October 25, 1904, in New York to an Austro-Hungarian father and a Polish mother. He joined the Disney studio on November 15, 1934, after having worked since 1923 for Paul Terry. During his first year at the Disney studio, he animated Clarabelle Cow in *Mickey's Fire Brigade*, a gingerbread boy and girl in *The Cookie Carnival*, a pair of black dolls in *Broken Toys*, and a bully rooster in *Cock O' the Walk*.

For *Snow White*, while he animated quite a few of the dwarfs, he will be remembered mostly for the way he gave true feelings to the unforgettable Grumpy. In *Pinocchio*, he handled the explosive puppeteer Stromboli. *Fantasia* offered him not one but two great challenges: the Sorcerer from the "Sorcerer's Apprentice" sequence and the evil Chernabog from "Night on Bald Mountain", probably his greatest achievement.

In the meantime, in 1938, Tytla had also returned briefly to shorts to supervise the animation of the Giant in *Brave Little Tailor*.

But Tytla did more than just villains. In *Dumbo*, he animated the main character, taking as reference his own son and creating some of the funniest, as well as some of the most moving, scenes in the feature.

In 1941, Bill Tytla followed his friend Art Babbitt and joined the traumatic strike at the Disney studio. After the strike, he continued working at Disney, but things were no longer the same. His assignments were less challenging. In 1943, he handled Pedro the baby plane and Jose Carioca, the parrot in *Saludos Amigos*; Hitler in *Reason and Emotion*; a witch and a Nazi teacher in *Education for Death*, and the climatic battle between the octopus and the American eagle in *Victory Through Air Power*. He left the studio that same year.

The next 25 years by contrast would be totally anticlimactic. He rejoined Paul Terry, then moved in 1944 to Paramount/Famous Studios where he directed *Popeye*, *Little Audrey*, and *Little Lulu* shorts. In 1950, he joined Tempo Productions as a director. In the mid 1950s, while still directing TV commercials in New York, Tytla was commuting on weekends to his farm in Connecticut. When his efforts at transforming that farm into a business failed in 1958, he headed his own company in New York, William Tytla Productions, Inc., directing more TV commercials.

The last four years of Bill's life saw him in increasingly poor health, and he passed away on December 31, 1968.

George Sherman interviewed Bill Tytla on May 13, 1968, the last time Bill was in California. The following is the result of this interview. Tytla was in extremely poor health at the time and had already had three previous strokes. His final one occurred seven-and-a-half months later. George Sherman says, "I knew he was ill. After hearing tales of this big full-of-life individual, I was surprised to see him bent and stuttering; obviously something was wrong. He still had the talent to animate, but he couldn't work fast enough, and today everything is speed—not quality, and get-it-out-in-a-damn-hurry."

This interview was first published in the magazine *Cartoonist PROfiles*, number 7, from September 1970. Cartoonist PROfiles' editor, Jud Hurd, was kind enough to allow its republication as part of the *Walt's People* series.

For the sake of consistency with the rest of the book, we have included complete questions in brackets before Bill's answers instead of short titles referring to the subjects of those answers.

....

George Sherman: [Could you tell us a few words about your] personal history?

Bill Tytla: I came to work for Walt Disney in 1934.

I was a high school dropout. I went to Paris to study. Paris was a base for branching out in all directions. Paul Terry contacted me there and asked me to return to New York and work for him. From there, I went to Disney's. I left in 1943 to return to Connecticut.

I first heard of Disney in 1929, in Paris. I went to a movie there and saw one of his shorts. I wondered who he was.

Later, I had the opportunity to watch some stolid Germans as they sat through a Disney short. They didn't laugh at all. Throughout the film they turned to each other and made a motion of a wheel turning by their ear. They thought he was screwy...they thought the man was "addled". They didn't understand him at all.

Some of the men came from New York. I was attending an art school in New York, and there I met Ted Sears. He wore his hair plastered down, and he talked out the side of his mouth. He wore a high collar and looked like a defrocked priest. But he walked along the hall dropping little nuggets of humor. In New York, I also first met Ben Sharpsteen. He tore out a page from a book on cartooning and gave it to me. I never forgot it—it was one of the most thoughtful things anybody ever did for me. Later on, I always remembered him from the old days. Some of the other men didn't like him—he was a hard taskmaster—but I always did. Because of what he did for me in New York.

Walt and Roy Disney knew of me because of what I did for Terry. They would look at Terry's productions and could recognize my animation. Roy would call me up whenever he was in New York, and finally in 1934 I went to the studio for the first time. It was an on-again, off-again romance until I flew west.

GS: [Do you recall your] first meeting with Walt Disney?

In 1934, I flew from New York to the Disney studio. The flight took 18 hours. Jesus, but I was impressed by the Disney studio. It was such a beautiful plant. By this time I knew all about Walt. I knew he animated well, and I believe in good animation.

I thought that Walt must be a great guy, and when I met him he lived up to everything I had anticipated. And he always retained that esteem in my mind.

His working conditions were terrific. He was miles ahead of the competition in all fields.

I returned to New York to tidy up my affairs and in November, 1934, started to work full time at the studio.

GS: [What were your responsibilities on] *Snow White and the Seven Dwarfs*?

Freddy Moore and I were responsible for the dwarfs. There were seven of them, all the same size, and only one (Dopey) who didn't have hair on his face. Each one was a separate color. We animated all seven of them at once.

On *Snow White*, Walt always gave us directions. We were all walking on tiptoes on that one. We didn't know what to expect. We were all full of all kinds of emotions.

Today, I know that the animation style differs for a feature, a short, or a commercial. But in those days, we weren't aware of the difference.

I first became aware of Walt on *Snow White*. I never saw much of him before that.

GS: [What about your work on] *Dumbo*?

This picture went very fast. It was the nature of the film to go very fast and get it out in a hurry. The baby Dumbo was mine.

GS: [Any special moments you remember from your work on] *Pinocchio?*

I had to animate one sequence in *Pinocchio*, and I gave it everything I had. There were several scenes in the sequence, and I showed my animation to the other animators. They all said "great" or "nothing else is needed" or "don't change a thing". I felt pretty good about it.

Finally, the time came for Walt to see it. He was subdued and even jolly in the sweat box. We ran the sequence, the lights went on, and we all waited to see what Walt would say.

He said, "That was a helluva scene *but*"—there's always that cruel *but* in there—"if anybody else had animated it, I would have passed it. But I expected something different from Bill."

Well, he sunk a ship with that remark. Understand, there was nothing mean in the way he said it. It was very natural. He was expecting something else from me, that's all.

It took a couple of weeks before I could work again. I was crushed. But one day I took up my pencil and started to draw again, differently. It was as if something hit me, and I started all over. This time when I showed it to Walt he said, "Great. Just what I was expecting!"

He never did explain what was wrong. It was as if in some magical way you would know [what was wrong].

GS: [How did you tackle your challenges on] *Fantasia?*

I animated the devil in "Night on Bald Mountain".

On all my animation I tried to do some research and look into the background of each character. [George Sherman's Note: Sort of like the Actors Studio which evolved years later.] So I did some reading about Moussorgsky.

Now, I'm Ukrainian, and Moussorgsky used terms I could understand. He talked about Chorni-Bok, the Black Art. Ukrainian folklore is based on Chorni-Bok. I related to this.

Walt had the knack of introducing you to your adversary. I don't think he knew of my background—actually, the director gave me the assignment, not Walt. But I remembered my background and studied up on Chorni-Bok. It's not related to American mythology but to European.

I used some of my background in the short [*Education for Death*]. I was given a German schoolmaster to animate. And I animated Hitler, in a scene where the hair fell down over his face and he'd use his lower lip as a funnel to blow away the hair.

At one point, one of my characters had to pick up a sword. I remembered my father, who was a Ukrainian cavalryman. I remembered the cavalry gesture as they brought their swords to a full salute. I used this gesture in animating the German. It was authentic—it was good animation.

GS: [Did you join] the strike [in 1941 due to the fact that you did not receive a] bonus on *Snow White*?

I cannot remember being promised a bonus. Even if I had, it would not have egged me on to extend myself.

I was for the company union, and I went on strike because my friends were on strike. I was sympathetic with their views, but I never wanted to do anything against Walt.

The food supplied by the union wasn't for me, so one lunch hour I went to a nearby greasy spoon for lunch. There was Walt in a booth. I went up to him, and we shook hands. I told him the strike was foolish and unnecessary. He asked me to return to his office with him to work out a solution. I was dressed in old clothes, so I asked to go home, shower, and change. We made an appointment for later that afternoon.

I drove to my home in La Canada, and my wife said that Walt had just called to cancel our meeting. Somebody had gotten to him and told him not to work with me. I wasn't an officer of the union, and I really couldn't speak for anybody anyway.

Later when the union officials wanted to meet with some of our men I went with them to the Hollywood Roosevelt Hotel. I introduced the men and left—I had no part in their discussions or meeting.

GS: [Any special memories of] Walt [you would like to share]?

We were sitting in a sweat box one day and I told Walt, "Give me something with some balls to it." His eyebrow shot up and—I can draw how he looked but not say it. He liked the phrase and he picked it up. Every so often I'd hear him use it.

Walt had trouble with the liquid "l". He always called me Weeyum. Never William. He'd say, "Wee-yum, whaddya know?" And I'd answer, "Nothing, until somebody tells me."

© 1970 George Sherman and Jud Hurd

Ken Anderson (1909–1993)

Interviewed by Paul F. Anderson in 1992

The "jack-of-all-trades". Good at animation, great at scene layout, character design, and art direction for movies and theme parks, Ken Anderson is considered by many as Disney's "tenth old man". He was without the shadow of a doubt one of the most influential artists at the Disney studio from the mid-1930s to the late 1970s.

Born near Seattle in 1909, he studied architecture there at the University of Washington, then won a scholarship which allowed him to study at the Ecole des Beaux Arts in Fontainebleau (France) and at the American Academy of Rome (Italy). When he returned from these studies in Europe in 1934, he worked for six weeks at MGM sketching sets for *The Painted Veil* and *What Every Woman Knows* before joining the Disney studio that same year.

His first special assignment: animating a moving background on the short *Three Orphan Kittens* (1935). After that project, he left animation to join the Layout Department that was headed at the time by Charles Philippi and Hugh Hennesy.

On *Snow White and the Seven Dwarfs*, all of his skills were put to good use: he animated scenes from the "party-in-the-dwarfs'-cottage" sequence, created layouts and sketches for the proposed "dream sequence", experimented with the multiplane camera, and built a model of the dwarfs' house to guide animators.

He served again as one of the art directors on both *Pinocchio* and *Fantasia* (on the first part of the "Pastoral Symphony" sequence), as well as on the short *Ferdinand the Bull* (1938).

For *The Three Caballeros* and *Song of the South*, he teamed up with Mary Blair, devising ways to adapt her unique style to the screen. Around the same time, he was credited as contributing to the stories on *Melody Time*, *So Dear to My Heart*, and *Cinderella*, and doing color styling on *Alice in Wonderland*.

In the early 1950s, he joined the newly created WED (today known as Walt Disney Imagineering). As an Imagineer, he was the principal designer on the Fantasyland "dark rides" and his many memorable projects included designing *Storybook Land* and the interior of the *Sleeping Beauty* castle. He was also one of the first artists to tackle the project that would later become the *Haunted Mansion*.

Returning to the animation medium, he worked again as production designer on *Sleeping Beauty*, then introduced the Xerography technique on *101 Dalmatians*, for which he served as solo production designer.

Virtually all the animated features that came out of the Disney Studio from that point on were unmistakably marked by his style. He served as art director on *Sword in the Stone* and tackled both art direction and character design on *The Jungle Book*, *The Aristocats*, *Robin Hood*, *The Rescuers*, and *Pete's Dragon*, for which he created Elliott.

One of the last projects he worked on was *Catfish Bend*, a proposed animated feature for which he did preliminary sketches.

Ken retired in 1978, became a Disney Legend in 1991, and died from a heart attack on December 13, 1993.

Paul F. Anderson conducted an exceptionally long series of interviews with Ken. The interview below is one of the early sessions in that series (tape 6 of a 34-tape oral history) and is presented here for the first time. It was transcribed by Jim Hill and Didier Ghez.

Paul F Anderson: Tell me the story of when Walt came to you about making your name famous.

Ken Anderson: That was in 1934, during my first days at the studio. He called me into his office and said "I have something that I want you to learn here. This is the *Walt Disney* studio. If you're thinking of making a name for yourself, then you'd better get the hell out of here now because the one thing we are selling here is 'Walt Disney'. Not because it's me. But because that's the name for the studio. And that's the place you work. That's all you have to do. Push this one name, Walt Disney". And he explained why it was that nobody got credits. It was all Walt Disney. "Because," he said, "that's what people remember. Walt Disney. We want them to remember that. We want it to mean something. If you can accept that, you're my man." And I thought that it was a very wonderful thing for him to do. Anybody working for him was put in an untenable position. But you had the joy of creating something for someone who you knew, and [if] he appreciated it, then it was damn good. And you found out how good it was when it was done. The concept really sold itself.

PA: So you were impressed by his straightforwardness. Had you given up your hopes of becoming the world's greatest architect?

I think I had. I think—even in 1949—while the guys were leaving the studio because of the time after the War, and there was a big transformation going on, everybody was deciding what they wanted to do. And

I thought: "You know, I could be a dentist. And I could work and fish and have a wonderful time in Oregon or Washington...."

PA: A dentist?!

Yeah, a dentist can work anywhere. But the lure of Disney was too great, and I never licked it. I had never known for sure if I was hired, I don't think he ever told anybody. Anytime I got a contract, it was all in favor of the studio. It would be for three years. But the studio had the whole say on how long you were going to work for him and what it was going to be for and all that stuff. And you slaved in spite of this contract you hated. But you thought it had to be done.

A little item about Walt: when he first met me, I was working on *Ferdinand the Bull*.

PA: Yes, that was a great story you told me. Tell me again.

I was working on *Ferdinand*. Well, Walt was gone, traveling in Europe and didn't know what was going on. And I was nuts to do this picture. Boy, this is a wonderful project, I thought. Because it is Spain, this hot country. And I lived there, I knew the country so well. I loved the hot Spanish colors. And I thought, "Wow. This is going to be a fantastic thing." But there was this guy who was the head of the background painters, Mique Nelson, who was not at all in sympathy with me. He didn't want me to do these things with all these hot, bright colors. And I said, "Come on, we gotta do it." And I had a friend among the background painters who supported me, his name was Claude Coats. He was quiet. In a quiet way, he said, "Yeah, I like the hot colors, I think we should do that, too." And so Claude believed me and he made some paintings but they were not nearly wild enough in color for me. But he thought that they'd get by Walt better. But they were far different from what had been done before. The way they were doing it, there would be a blue sky that could be pulled through in a pan with a couple of clouds. So everything was tints. And they were very careful not to use much color.

The word was out that Walt hated purple and that Walt hated painting. And this background man was dead set against what we were trying to do with all of these bright, hot colors. And he got so mad and so piqued because we were going ahead and doing it anyway. And he said, "Well, Walt's gonna kill you guys. You guys are gonna get it. I'm not going to support you." On and on. But we were writing him off. You see, we were just saying: "We know what we are doing." So we went ahead and did it. We got the whole thing done. And we were just in the process of looking at it and admiring it. It looked pretty good to Claude and myself. Well, Walt came back and he saw it—not with me and Claude in the room—but with the head of the backgrounds. Walt loved it. He thought this background painter that had hated it had done it, so he gave him $60 a week raise. He said "Gee, that's marvelous, Mique. Keep that sort of thing up. That's good thinking. You really did it." And no, nothing at all for Claude and me! It was six months later when Walt found out that Mique didn't really do it, that Claude and I had done it. And he gave us a raise. He didn't take Mique's away. But he gave us a raise.

PA: I understand that you were the one who was responsible for Herb Ryman coming to the Disney studio from MGM.

That's right. I was working in the art department making story sketches at MGM, and Herbie was really big at MGM then. We would get a plan from the director, who would show us around where the cameras were going to be set. We would plan the whole background. How they worked, the placement, and so forth. Make it into a picture, using their provisions for the cameras, whatever lenses they were using. We decided what needed to be drawn and would make drawings to illustrate these various positions for the director. The director had to be able to look at these drawings and say "That's going to be here. This is going to be there. And this is the way it's going to look." And I used to just love working with Herb Ryman and another art director at MGM, Harold Miles, these two guys were just the greatest artists. So I used to sneak off at every chance I had, and go back to see their work. They had this work all pinned up around the room. And I just loved the stuff. That was the amount of knowing him that I did at MGM.

After I was gone for a month from MGM because they didn't have work for me, I needed a job and I went to Disney. Herbie was still working at MGM. Later, at Disney, I was working on some scenes where the backgrounds were so important, and I could not forget Herbie and his wonderful work. I thought "Gee that guy would be terrific over here." But he was making a lot of money at MGM and Disney couldn't compete with that. But I knew that Herbie wasn't happy, as he hated the nepotism at that studio. These nephews of the chairman would come in and tear your drawings up. So I figured I'd talk to Herb. I said, "Hey, would you like to work for Disney, I really think that I can get you in." And he said, "Well, I don't know. I'd like to get out of here." I told Walt, "Gee, I sure met a great artist over at MGM and I think that he'd be wonderful working here. I don't know what he would do. But I suppose he could work in story." And Walt was very sympathetic right off the bat. So Walt hired him. I don't know what he paid, but he got him over to the studio.

PA: I want to talk about your typical day at the Disney Studios while you were working on *Snow White*. You told me that you would start your layout for a scene after you had been to the story meetings where things were pinned down. After you worked a full day on your layout, would you leave right at five o'clock or did you get excited about the layout and work on it into the night?

Yes, through the night.

PA: What was that like?

We worked until midnight many nights. We worked on weekends. We didn't know that there was another picture in mind. That was the one picture. That was our one effort.

PA: Did you eat? Would you take time to say run across the street and have dinner?

Yes.

PA: Did you go with other friends at the studio?

Sometimes. But most often you just cut the other guys out. You were busy creating.

PA: Speaking of creating, what did you find to be the most creative for you, putting together the layout, or the actual ideas that might sprout from a story meeting?

The stories. The story ideas. The things that would go into making the layout, then the creation of the layout was the summation. Using all of these ideas that you came up with in story that you could use in the layout.

PA: So was midnight a pretty honest assessment of when you'd look at your watch and say "Oh, no. I've been doing this layout ever since I got up this morning! Time to go home."

I never went by the clock. Even when I had quit for the night, I was still working. I would go home and I'd think about what I was doing. It's a wonder that I didn't have car wrecks over and over because I'd be thinking about all this *Snow White* stuff. And carry off into a different world. So I'd grab some sleep and wake up and go to work again. It would be some time, maybe in the morning. But we didn't have a time that we had to clock in. There was no punching of clocks at the beginning of *Snow White*. That came later.

PA: After the strike?

Yes. But on *Snow White* you made your own hours. You would come when you wanted to. And we were always there. There were always guys who were there.

PA: So when you were at the studio late into the night, it wasn't always because of a deadline, it was because you really loved what you were doing.

Oh, yeah. Loved it. I just loved it.

PA: So how did your wife, Polly, act with you coming home so late? And so often? Was she supportive?

Oh, yes, very much. Because she had worked there. And knew some of the things I was going through.

PA: So when you'd come home at—like say midnight, would you wake her up and run all of these ideas by her?

Sometimes. And I didn't have to wake her up sometimes. I'd come home and she was awake. Did I ever tell you the story about her working there?

PA: No.

You know, there was a state law at the time that men and women could not be married and they could not be a family and work in the same business. So it was illegal for Polly and me to work at Disney. I never brought her around to the studio when I was working there, so nobody knew we were married. I had this idea for her to approach the studio for a job. I did some artwork for her, which consisted of a series of illustrations of fashion design, which a man would not be used to, not be thinking of having. And I was worried that maybe people would recognize my drawing, you know like when people recognize your handwriting, so I drew everything for Polly with my left hand. So she had this nice, colorful portfolio full of fashion drawings that she took to the studio and they were astounded. What an artist she was. Just wonderful. They hired her, and they hired her for more than I was getting! I was making $15 a week and she was making $18! It did not last too long, as I got a $4 a week raise. They were very careful back then with their raises.

PA: Did they ever discover that you were married?

No. In fact, we were keeping it very quiet because we knew the seriousness of the thing. We'd both be canned. And neither of us would ever be able to get a job at the studio again.

PA: When was that?

It was the first year after I had been there...after the whole studio had closed for vacation, which happened around 1933. After that, Polly and I were both there.

PA: How long after that did Polly work at the Studio?

About two or three years.

PA: Did they ever find out that you two were married?

They never found out! She left several months before Sue [Ken and Polly's first daughter] was born. They knew at the studio that she was pregnant, and they were asking [laughter] "Now how did that happen? Who is she married to?" She had gone by her maiden name, so nobody knew.

PA: So in the following years as you got closer to Walt, and he might come over for dinner, or perhaps he saw you and Polly out at a restaurant, did he ever recognize her?

He never did, and we were always very quiet about it. That was a time that both of us remember. And treasure. Polly enjoyed working at the studio and even kept some of the bits and pieces of all the scenes she painted. She also did some inking.

PA: Back to *Snow White*, on your layout work do you have any recollection of Walt coming in and saying "I like what you're doing?"

Never did. I wondered if he liked what I was doing for twenty years. He never ever came in and said "Hey, you're doing great." It wasn't his style to compliment people. He might compliment you through another person. For instance, one of my layout friends would hear that "Ken Anderson is sure doing a good job."

PA: As the deadline grew closer and closer for *Snow White*, were there days that you were working Saturdays, Sundays, 12 hours a day straight through?

Oh, yeah. Many of them. *Snow White* was the big enterprise in our lives and we knew it was a feature. It was sort of the first feature, the only feature in animation that had ever really been tried. And we knew how important it would be to us, to ourselves. But we never even considered the future beyond this picture. It was what we were going to do. We were going to finish this up and get back to the rest of our lives and live off of the love of what we'd done. So it never occurred to us to hold our breath or anything. We just worked as many hours as we could stay awake.

PA: Since the folks in Hollywood were being pretty negative and calling it "Disney's Folly", what were your feelings about *Snow White* at the time?

Oh, it was wonderful. The picture was wonderful. And everything that we were doing was wonderful. And the people had to love it. It was just great. And we were trying to make it as good as Walt talked it. Because Walt gave us the whole Hollywood description of what he wanted. That was marvelous. If we had been able to do that—we tried, but we couldn't come up with a film as great as the thing he talked—I'm sure that it would have been even better than it was. But we knew that it was going to be good. Because it was just turning out great.

PA: So you had faith in it?

Absolutely.

PA: When a lot of people at the time didn't.

In fact, we tacked up the posters around Los Angeles. The studio didn't have the money to really promote it. They had these little square posters that were a foot wide and eighteen inches tall. They were green and white with Snow White and the dwarfs. We had a bunch of these posters and tacks, and we went all over Hollywood, all over Los Angeles in our cars, tacking these things up.

PA: Who else did that?

Oh, everybody. We wanted everybody to see it. "Hey, look at what we did. This film." So then there came the premiere of the film. It was a big deal. We all had monkey suits the first night. We were wearing these, we were really dressed up in clothes that weren't ours. We were standing around, trying to listen to what the big shots were saying. And these stars were all coming. We were looking at these stars. And they were coming to this thing to see it and they were pretty off-hand about it. They came "Oh, what the hell. It's a goddamn cartoon. We wouldn't waste any time on this damn thing or not if it was up to us to do it." And so they were kind of put upon to do this thing. And they came, they walked in the theatre, did this kind of down their nose thing. And they filled the theatre.

When they left, they were all talking about the story. In fact, you can't really begin to convey what they felt. Because they were astounded. They stood and they clapped and they had a terrific time at the end of the thing. And they were all kids again. These people were just moved by this thing, by this cartoon. They could not understand it. We were never prepared for this type of reception. And—boy—they were crowding around Walt. And each of us. They crowded all around, "What did you do?" And such and such. We're standing out there in the foyer and these people just went on and on and on and on about this marvelous picture. And I—for one—and I know everybody must have felt the same way, was thrilled.

PA: So after you had received all of the praise at the premiere, what was it like back at the studio? I know there was a team working on *Bambi*, but what about all of those coming off of *Snow White*. Obviously, everyone was happy, but what were people saying? I guess I'm asking when did it dawn on people that *Snow White* was done?

It took a good two weeks. We went back to the studio and had nothing to do. And we didn't do anything, either. We just came back, there was nothing to do. We lapped it up. We loved the wonderful praise. And we thought "Well, it's all over." And we got to thinking that "Walt's got to tell us another story." And we waited for him to tell us another story just like he did with *Snow White*. I'm sure it was different for each person, but for me, it took at least two weeks to realize that I had to do something else. But nobody was pushing us into doing anything. Some of the guys around the studio were getting itchy-pants and they got going right away with all kinds of ideas for stories. But none of them were like *Snow White*, you know really great stories. It finally kind of dawned on me, it must have been a month or so, that I thought "Gee, we better get to work and do something." The problem is we couldn't really conceive of anything that could compete with *Snow White*. How could we possibly top that? Well, it was Ben Sharpsteen's idea to do *Pinocchio*. We weren't really sold on it at first, but eventually we did get sold on the idea. They invited Gustav Tenggren, who had already worked on *Snow White*, to come in and make key sketches. Which he did, and we loved those sketches. He was a European and those were things he knew as a boy—he knew those places.

PA: What did you first do on *Pinocchio*?

First of all, I started working with Tenggren and looking at his stuff. We wanted to make something better than we had with *Snow White*, so we needed to utilize all of our talent and everything we had to translate to the screen what Tenggren was doing. There was a big background of the city where Geppetto lived, with little houses and everything all over. It would fill the whole section of this living room—beautifully drawn. We had to plot how the camera would roam all over this background. When we photographed it, there would be no cuts, it'd just be moving all around all the time with the camera. It gave this wonderful picture of reality. On that, I had some things I did on Geppetto's house. I liked some of Tenggren's drawings, and some of them I didn't care so much for. So some would work and some wouldn't. So I was exploring the house and all the different drawings and the city and the town and little Pinocchio going to school. There were all kinds of things to explore. And I was taking my time to do that.

PA: For your research on Geppetto's house and the European village, what type of research did Walt provide for you? You always hear how Walt had a complete collection of *National Geographics* for research.

You'd think he would, wouldn't you? You'd think he would provide us with material, but he never did. He expected us to find those things and show him. He didn't really have anything to show anybody. In fact, he didn't have any story or anything else for *Pinocchio*. It wasn't until Frank Thomas and some of the other animators did some scenes of little Pinocchio unable to walk, being dangled around, and so forth, that we got going. Those things kind of led the way. And Walt began to get excited about the picture and then the animators did. And there still was no story other than the original story of *Pinocchio*, but we weren't following it terribly closely.

PA: So what kind of research and material did you go after for this European village and Geppetto's house? You had spent time in Europe studying architecture, you must have made use of that experience?

I did. And that architecture was very familiar to me because I had studied that sort of thing in school. And I knew all of those scenes. I didn't know them as well as Tenggren did, who grew up with it, but I knew them well. In fact, I knew them well enough to appreciate what Tenggren was doing with them. Of course, he wasn't involved enough in the process of the picture to relate them to the storytelling. So they weren't telling the story of the picture.

PA: Did you attend some of the early story meetings on *Pinocchio*?

Oh, yes. You bet. The story slowly started to develop from those meetings.

PA: Do you have any recollections of Walt showing up for these meetings and showing the same enthusiasm for *Pinocchio* as he did for *Snow White*?

I never saw that same enthusiasm from him ever. But he showed up and he had some great ideas and he sure as hell sparked the meetings.

PA: So you were doing layout still? I mean, even though you were working with Tenggren and going to story meetings?

Not at this time. I was just doing story sketches. Mostly story sketches, but some character sketches and drawings. As time went on, I got more and more into the drawing of characters and the backgrounds, and paid very little attention to making the layouts.

PA: We all know that Ward Kimball got Jiminy Cricket; other than that, did others get a specific character or were they given to a team of people? If so, what characters did you do?

Both. I worked on the Blue Fairy. Frank Thomas, Ollie Johnston, and Milt Kahl, they all got characters in *Pinocchio* to do—as much as Kimball had. But they never received the adulation that Ward had received, because he had the character that everybody idolized.

PA: I know of your enthusiasm for *Snow White*. Obviously, your interest in architecture and the time you spent in Europe should have provided that enthusiasm for *Pinocchio*. Did it?

It grew into that, it grew into a great interest. Though I still didn't think that it was another *Snow White*. I don't think I could have ever felt that. But *Pinocchio* was a challenge to visualize and make good drawings on.

PA: After the story work was being completed, did you go back to doing animation or layout with *Pinocchio*?

No, I built a model of Stromboli's wagon. It saved a lot in animation because you could plan it out, the movement and everything. You could photograph it and then get a black-and-white frame print on a cel. And you would have an animated scene. It would bounce over the pavement, down the road. It was quite interesting to plan this thing and then to get this all done. It was fun to do. And then I had to combine that with the interior scenes where there are characters hanging and it was going by outside. It was pretty complicated.

PA: You did a model of Geppetto's house, too, didn't you?

Yes, but it was never used, or it was never used in total. Various rooms were used. And it was made in pieces so it would join together or pull apart so you could photograph different angles.

PA: During the production of *Pinocchio*, did you see the same kind of devotion there was on *Snow White*, you know working twelve, sixteen hour days?

Not as much as there was on *Snow White*.

PA: Interesting.

I still think that *Snow White* was the best we ever did.

PA: In a way, that is somewhat ironic, that the first was the best. Why do you feel it was the best?

Mostly because of Walt's involvement, and his telling us the story so well.

He told the whole story as if it was something he had been a part of. It was told with such vigor and strength that we got it. Every one of us got the picture. And we were—all of us—doing the same thing. Working and trying to come up with the same result that he had when he was telling it.

PA: So Walt's enthusiasm was what made it the best and pulled it off for everyone?

Yes. And he didn't have that for *Pinocchio*. He had the right ideas and so on and so forth and here and there. But not like he was with *Snow White,* where he saw the whole thing.

PA: So after *Pinocchio* came out, what were your feelings about the film?

I thought it was pretty good. It wasn't *Snow White*. And there are people that think it is better than *Snow White*. You know, they thought that this was the best one yet.

PA: People at the studio?

Yes. And everywhere. I was amazed because I didn't think so. But there was this enormous concept for the film. There was this huge whale, and the water was marvelous. It was very well done. But it didn't have the heart that *Snow White* had.

PA: We are getting fairly close to the studio move to Burbank while you were working on *Pinocchio*?

That's right.

PA: Maybe you could talk a little bit about your feelings during that transition from the Hyperion studio to the Burbank studio. I understand you made an offer to Walt as far as helping with the architecture on the new studio?

Did you know about that? That I'd made this offer to Walt?

PA: Yes.

I don't know that it was ever written up. Having had this architectural background and having been proved successful and the winning of the scholarship for Fontainebleau and a couple of years in Paris, and all over Europe, I thought: "Why shouldn't Walt partake of this? He can have it." So I wrote him a nice note. Said that in no way would I lose work, lose sight of my work. I would keep that first in my mind. But here I had this six years of education in architecture and I was very successful. I thought this was a good chance for Walt to utilize me because I was in the animation end of things. And I knew I could plan animation things that were ideal for animators. Boy, that was a death knell. I never should have done that. Because evidently—thinking back at what he must have thought—you know: "Who in the hell is this Ken Anderson smart-ass son-of-a-bitch who wants to do my building? He doesn't have to do that. He's not going to have anything to do with it." So he invited the whole studio to see the plans, the place for the new studio, except for me. And they had the architect Kem Weber there to talk to everyone, he did all the stuff and all the desks. And everyone was out there at the new studio where it is now and I sat alone back at the Hyperion studio.

PA: On any of the other pictures did Walt ever approach that same enthusiasm he had for *Snow White*?

Yeah. *Fantasia.* He came close. He really felt *Fantasia.*

PA: I think that kind of broke his heart, too, the way it was received.

That's right. But he learned—eventually—that if it's a good thing and it was done by Walt Disney's group, after the years go by, it will be a hit. Then you're alright.

PA: Seeing as how there were only ten months between the release of *Pinocchio* and *Fantasia,* you must have been doing double duty?

I think I finished *Pinocchio* before I started on *Fantasia.* I don't think I was working on two pictures at once.

PA: You and I have listened to a lot of classical music together, and I know of your love for it. Did that inspire you on *Fantasia*?

Boy, it sure did. That was terrific. Though controversial. The best yet.

PA: Oh, the best yet?

Yeah. Of all of them. It was a wonderful music to animate to.

PA: So when did you first hear about *Fantasia*?

Well, when I heard about it, it was already in production. In fact, a lot of it was well done when Walt decided that certain scenes needed to be added as the picture progressed. It didn't all happen and it wasn't all pre-ordained in one fell swoop. It took a whole lot of roads. And "The Sorcerer's Apprentice" sequence was the first. Originally, it was going to be just that. And that was a very good thing. Walt was always looking for more. He was trying to figure out how to make a feature out of it.

And he began to find other pieces of music that would work, and he had Leopold Stokowski to help him. They finally came up with the music that we were going to use for this thing. In the meantime, I had been finishing the picture I was working on, which was *Pinocchio,* and Walt said, "Hey, you know what you guys gotta do is to come over to this thing here." Beethoven. And he turned on the Beethoven and we were really stuck. Because the whole picture was waiting for us to finish Beethoven. We got Beethoven to do when the rest of the picture was almost finished in the beginning. We started working on this "Pastoral Symphony", and it had a lot of different characteristics. Mermaids. Pegasuses.

PA: Walt was really keen on finding out what talents and interests his people had. Did he ever approach you on the classical music aspect? Since that was a love of yours?

No. I don't know as he ever knew that. He might have, just by our talking.

PA: Were you excited about Beethoven and the "Pastoral Symphony"?

I was. I didn't think that it was the strongest one they had. I thought: "Oh, golly. They'll do it. But it's got some great music." But I didn't see how we were going to come up to the music with our guy that crosses the sky and all that stuff. And there were these centaurs and centaurettes. Which I thought was kind of namby-pamby. We did everything as fast as we could and as well as we could. And beautiful scenes of the flying horses in the trees and all this stuff. But the only gutsy scene was with Bacchus.

PA: Did you sit in your office and shut your eyes and listen to the music?

Oh, all the time.

PA: What a great job!

I loved that thing. Day and night. I lived that music. I loved it.

PA: So you did some animation. Did you do any layout?

Yes. A little.

PA: Did you work on the story?

Oh, a lot of the story.

PA: What would a typical story meeting be like for the "Pastoral" in *Fantasia*? When everybody interprets music differently?

That's right.

PA: How do you make order come from that chaos?

Well, you had to make drawings and paintings. You'd make these little sketches you could do fairly quickly that would tell far more than you could do with words.

PA: I see the tape is coming to an end. Ready for a break?

Yes. Thanks.

Jack Hannah (1913–1994)

Interviewed by Jim Korkis in July 1978 and May 1981, plus additional conversations until 1994

John Frederick (Jack) Hannah was born in Nogales, Arizona, on January 5, 1913. He passed away on June 11, 1994, at St. Joseph's Hospital in Burbank, California. He was honored as a Disney Legend in 1992. After attending schools in California, he moved to Los Angeles to take art courses at Otis and Chouinard schools in 1931. His first jobs were designing posters for Foster and Kleiser as well as for Hollywood theaters.

He joined the Disney studio in 1933 and spent five years as an animator, another five years in the Story Department where he was teamed with Carl Barks as a story team, and then close to twenty years as a director of animated shorts. He worked on well over a hundred cartoons with Donald Duck, Chip 'n' Dale, and Humphrey the Bear among many Disney characters. Eight of the cartoons he directed were nominated for Academy Awards.

He also directed fourteen hour-long Disney television shows, many of which featured Walt Disney interacting with Donald Duck. He left the Disney studio in 1959 and worked briefly at the Walter Lantz studio, where he was also responsible for directing the live-action openings of the *Woody Woodpecker* television show.

Jack returned to Disney in the 1960s to work as a story consultant on live-action films. In 1975, Hannah was asked by the Disney studio to develop and take charge of the School of Character Animation at the California Institute of the Arts. He worked there for eight years.

In addition, Jack was a skilled landscape artist and his paintings were displayed in galleries throughout the West. Jack was considered one of the major influences on Donald Duck's animated personality, since he worked on the Duck as an animator, storyman, and director.

The following is a selection from interviews Jim Korkis did with Jack in July 1978 and May 1981, as well as bits and pieces of additional conversations Jim had with Jack up to 1994.

Jim Korkis: How did you first join the Disney Studio?

Jack Hannah: I was seeking work in the commercial art field during the Depression. I went into an art agency with my portfolio and there was this guy who said to me, "Why don't you try Disney?" I replied that I wasn't a cartoonist but a commercial artist. He kept insisting, and said, "You'd be surprised. Walt takes young fellows that have some talent." With fear in my heart, I went out there and turned in my portfolio. I waited for about a week or two. I was finally called on the phone by Ben Sharpsteen. Sharpsteen at that time was reviewing incoming talent, and he asked me to come in for a two weeks' tryout. That two weeks' tryout ended up in thirty years of work at Disney.

JK: Did you start as an in-betweener?

I started immediately as an in-betweener, as all the young fellows did. I started January 31, 1933. The going rate when you started was $16.00 a week, but Walt had an incentive plan. You were under contract, but quarterly you'd get a two-dollar raise. I believe I started at the studio too young. I had just turned twenty years old, and I don't think I was mature enough to grasp the real meaning of what animation really was. I sort of tore into it like any young buck would without really thinking too much. However, I was pretty well thought of because I was moved from in-betweening to assistant very quickly.

JK: What was some of your first animation?

I assisted such outstanding animators as Norm Ferguson, Dick Huemer, Ham Luske, Les Clark, and several others. Usually, they would give their assistant a scene or two out of their sequence to animate. You would not only go along and clean up all of their animation, but often you'd get a scene or two of your own to do that fit into their sequence. This way, you learned gradually how to put a piece of animation together. When I assisted Ferguson, he animated very loosely, so I progressed faster because I had to follow up the toughest guy. He was very loose and had a terrific sense of flow. When you picked up his roughs, you were practically starting from scratch. He'd take two or three short scenes and hand them to his assistant to animate. Then, after he viewed the pencil tests, he turned it in with his sequence. He'd make comments, but it removed a lot of pressure and eased me into doing full animation. I worked on *Three Little Pigs* and several shorts. The first scenes I animated were in *Shanghaied* in 1934, such as the scene where Mickey is dueling with Pete with the swordfish. In *The Band Concert*, I animated that bit where during the storm the benches get up and start running away. I animated a bat sequence in *The Old Mill* where a series of bats woke up and yawned and flew out.

JK: How did you get involved with the Donald Duck shorts?

Jack King joined the studio while I was an assistant. He came from New York and was working on doing a new series of cartoons featuring Donald Duck. I was picked to join this crew as a full-fledged animator. It was exciting. I consider my work at that period of time as "in the middle". I didn't knock 'em dead with my animation, but Jack King always seemed pleased with what I would come up with. About this time, the *Snow White* excitement was stirring up the studio, and Walt started looking all over the country for fresh talent. Several "middle of the roaders" like myself were pegged to be moved aside for some of this new talent coming in. Even then, I knew that I was never going to be one of the top animators. My talent seemed to lie in a different direction.

JK: So you moved over to the Story Department?

At the time, they would hand out scripts of stories, looking for story ideas, and I was beginning to pick up a little extra money submitting gags. We'd be paid anywhere between $2.50 to $5.00 if a gag was used. This was good spending money on the side. Harry Reeves, who was in charge of the Story Department, stepped in about the time they were going to dislodge me as an animator. He invited me to transfer into the Story Department. The transition was made, but it wasn't as smooth as I make it sound. It really did hurt because I really did love animation.

JK: What was the Story Department like at that time?

They had a little apartment building in the back of the Hyperion lot. It was an old apartment house, and I guess Walt had either bought it or rented it for the Story Department. This was where I first met Carl Barks, who, of course, was not only a fine storyman but later became quite famous as a comic-book writer and artist. Carl was already a storyman there. At first, I was still grieving over the fact that I was no longer an animator, and all I was doing was some story sketching. But when I began to see how a story was being put together and built, I began to get more and more interested in it. Just about that time, we moved to the new studio in Burbank and they set Carl and me up with Jack King as his two storymen. So we were an official team from that time on. At the old studio, I worked with two or three different crews.

JK: What was Carl Barks like to work with?

Carl and I got along fine. Carl had done a lot of magazine work before he came to the studio. I think he liked that kind of work and was getting sick of the regime type of work he had to do for Disney. At the studio, it was definitely a teamwork effort and Carl was an individual. He seemed more comfortable working alone. But I really loved working with him.

We'd get a Sears and Roebuck catalog and see a picture of a tractor and that might give us the springboard for a whole short about the Duck on a farm. Ideas came from everywhere. Anyway, we would sit and discuss a situation and build up a section together. Then we'd divide it up and work separately on it. Later, we'd come back together to work on the storyboard. I'll give you an example. In *Truant Officer Donald*, Carl came up with that idea of Donald pulling the covers back and finding the three roast chickens with the nephews' hats on. My idea was having the nephew come down on a rope dressed like an angel. By the way, Harry Reeves hated that sequence where Donald thinks he's cooked Huey, Dewey, and Louie. Reeves thought it was too gruesome.

Carl had to be Carl. He couldn't sit down and share ideas in a story as easily as a lot of other people could. Everything he came up with was original. He didn't rely on the stockpile of gags that some people keep up in their heads, like Frank Tashlin did. "Tish Tash" could recall every gag he had ever heard and could just pull them out when he needed them. Carl couldn't do that. He and I got along fine, though. It may have had something to do with the fact that I was younger than Carl. He was older, and maybe he was more grown up and I was more juvenile, but when we weren't working on a story, I'd spend my time down in the commissary having a Coke and checking out the young girls, like the cute waitresses Walt had hired. Carl was a real workhorse. He'd still be back at his desk working away. He was always a bit of a loner, but not in an unfriendly sense, and he sometimes just had to work alone to do his best.

JK: The two of you did the first original Donald Duck comic book?

Elinor Packer, through John Rose[1], wanted someone to do this sixty-four page Donald Duck comic-book story called *Donald Duck Finds Pirate Gold*. I wasn't aware of it being a rejected Duck cartoon. I only saw the typed script by Bob Karp. He had typed out all the descriptions and the dialogue. At the time we were doing the comic book, neither Carl nor I had any idea that this was a proposal for a feature. It certainly seems strange that we never heard [of it], because along with Jack King, we were directly responsible for all the Duck shorts coming out of the studio. Still, if it were being developed as a feature, somebody may have felt it wasn't any of our business because we were just doing the shorts and this was a feature, so it would involve an entirely different group of people. They certainly never told us.

Carl and I said we'd do it because the money sounded good to us. We

---

1 Two executives from Whitman publishing who produced Disney comics for the DELL label.

each took thirty-two pages and did it at home. We only got together when necessary for the hook-ups to make sure we were drawing the same kitchen on the ship, etc. [Hannah drew pages 3, 4, 6-11, 41-64.] This had to be around 1942, I guess. I'm guessing I penciled about a page and a half to two pages a weekend. We would draw it up in blue pencil, and then it would have to be seen by the publishing company before we went ahead with the inking. The inking went quicker than the penciling, and I can't recall that there were any major changes we had to make on our blue-pencil stuff. Carl and I had several meetings on the weekends so that the props we were drawing looked the same and that the room setting would be the same. There would be the same pots on the stove or that kind of thing. We didn't have any difficulty synchronizing our style. We both fell into it easily, and I think we were both surprised at how close the drawing was, especially since we were doing it in two different homes.

After all, when we did story sketches for the shorts, we had our own individual ways of drawing the story, and both ways seemed to get the job done. Sometimes, because I had an interest in directing, I seemed to have paid more attention to shading or detailing, simply because I wanted to get the idea across to a director as clearly as possible. So, in some ways, it was a real surprise to see the comic-book work drawn so similar that it would be hard to tell which one of us drew the page.

We never did any of the actual work on the story at the studio. We may have discussed a story question at the studio, but that was infrequent at best. I never realized I had done so many other comic-book stories on my own until you showed me some of the pages and I immediately recognized them as mine. Those stories are definitely my work. I can tell by the way the Duck is drawn and by some of the things in the backgrounds. Little things like the position of a hand or a foot are dead giveaways. I can't recall ever being given any guidelines on how to do this work, and I'm sure I would have remembered if I had been. It was just an easy way to pick up some extra money.

I probably stopped doing comic books because I had to go back East for awhile for family business. The publisher gave Carl and me a lot of copies of *Pirate's Gold*. My kids tore 'em up. I still have a personal copy, but it's in less than mint shape. If I had known, I would have locked it away in a safe somewhere so the light couldn't get to it.

I did another comic story with Carl, *Pluto Saves the Ship*, which we cranked out together over a hot weekend without air conditioning, and a handful by myself, including *Donald Duck and the Pirates*, which was sort of a shortened re-do of *Pirate's Gold* for a Cheerios giveaway thing. I stopped doing the comic-book work when the studio started gearing up for war work.

JK: What was the new studio in Burbank like when you first moved there?

It was a complete change. Absolutely complete. The atmosphere was different. Walt tried something that didn't work. He put a secretary out at the front of each unit to answer all phone calls. He had a big soda fountain downstairs that catered room service to all units. All you had to do was pick up a phone and say, "Send up a double chocolate malt and a tuna sandwich." Anytime of the day or night, you could call and it would arrive with a cute little waitress in a fancy outfit. This was unbelievable, but it didn't work because people would abuse it. It was just too good a thing. Walt would go by downstairs in the middle of the day and he would see the same people sitting there having a cup of coffee or whatever. They'd be sitting there half the day instead of working. Walt finally blew up and the whole thing was thrown out. The whole set-up. All those cute young things.

JK: How was the Story Department set up at this time?

We'd develop a story with a crew of two storymen. At certain points, we'd call in two or three other groups for gag sessions. It was real teamwork in those gag sessions. You could either use all or part of what was suggested, or just throw it out completely. Roy Williams seldom came up with a complete story, but he was exceptionally good as a spot gag man.

JK: How did you get your first taste at directing?

You'll notice in my story credits with Carl that near the end of them, you'll see an awful lot of Army themes with Pete as the sergeant and the Duck as the dumb recruit. The studio was gearing up for the war. There was a picture that they gave to Jack King about a housewife saving fat for the war effort [*Out of the Frying Pan into the Firing Line* (1942)]. I don't know why they were supposed to save this grease. Maybe it was to make the enemy slip on it. Somebody told me it helped in the making of explosives. There were all kinds of these films being made. Anyway, Jack King wasn't interested in the mechanical part of this picture. You know, showing all these cooking fats and stuff going down a funnel and things like that. So he gave me a little section to direct, and I just loved it. Just to be able to do something. That was my first little piece of direction.

JK: Didn't you get to direct some training films on your own?

At this time, I had to go back to Wisconsin on family business, and when I returned to the Studio, Carl had quit and become a comic-book artist. It was at this time that the war came, and practically overnight there were no more theatrical cartoons being made at the studio. Or so it seemed. It seemed like it was all war work.

I was given a chance to direct training films. Mine were mainly for the Navy. I worked with the exploder mechanism of the torpedo, and I worked with stuff like the range finder on the torpedo plane. This work was very exacting and interesting, and I had to take several trips down to North Island in San Diego and work right with the torpedo planes. I don't really know how many training films I made during the war, but those were my first directing assignments.

JK: What happened after the war?

After the war was over, I went back to being a storyman. But without Carl, I just felt kind of lost. I was told of a young storyman, Bill Berg, who later developed into a very good storyman, who was struggling with a story. Hal Adelquist, who was now the head of the Story Department, asked me if I would go down and help him out with this story, and I did. I got it filled with a lot of personality bits which I always believed were more important in a story than just a series of gags. I went to Hal and said, "I'd just love to direct this. As much as I like Jack King, I can't see him directing these personality sequences." Carl and I always were disturbed that King put one of our stories onto the screen without looking for further development in the personalities of the characters. I just knew I could do this cartoon which was called *Donald's Off Day*.

Finally, after asking repeatedly for the chance, the word came back from Walt implying "Go ahead; let him hang himself." It was that type of attitude. I got a secretary, got an assistant, and started directing it. I met Walt in the hall one day and he asked, "How's it going?" I replied, "Fine, but if I don't get started on another cartoon, I'll have to put all my costs on this picture and it's going to run it over budget. I need another short to start on while this one is going through production." I'm certain that Walt had looked at that short either at home or in a projection room because I knew Walt better than to believe he'd just take my word for it. The next thing I knew, Adelquist came up to me and told me Walt had said it was okay to pick up another short to direct. So I picked up another one, and ended up directing cartoons for Disney for the next seventeen years.

JK: What were some of the changes in the Donald Duck shorts that occurred when you became a director?

We began looking for foils for the Duck. Naturally, his three nephews were always available. You've got to give a storyman an outlet for a new line of gags. It was natural that the Duck would have a girlfriend, so Daisy came along. Anything to open up story possibilities.

That's why the nephews were there. For a while, somebody came up with the idea that it would be clever to have the three nephews say one line of dialog with all three of them sharing in the sentence. One nephew would say the first two words, the next would say the middle of the sentence, and the third would finish it up. I put a stop to this because it ruined all sense of timing and you couldn't go on and carry through a gag. You'd have to stop and wait for each nephew to say his lines and you couldn't incorporate the dialogue in the action as well that way. We got each nephew saying an individual line all by himself. Jack King was never noted for his timing, so I guess it didn't bother him, but I got rid of it.

A lot of directors gave the animators more say in timing. I never did that. I timed every foot I directed. I don't care how good the animator was. To me, it was the most important part of the directing—the timing, the pacing, the pauses. While Donald and his nephews worked well together, we needed variety in our material, so we tried a variety of characters. The Aracuan bird, who was introduced earlier in *The Three Caballeros*, was one of our first attempts. There was a series with a beetle named Bootle Beetle. My wife knew a race horse in Pomona named Beetle Bootle, and I just switched it around. Working with these types of characters led up to Chip 'n' Dale.

JK: How were the chipmunks developed?

I believe Gerry Geronimi did a picture with two impish little chipmunks that just squeaked and chattered with a speeded-up soundtrack, but no words. He used them with Pluto. They were the forerunners of Chip 'n' Dale. I wanted to use them with the Duck, but with a little more personality put into them. So we decided to put words in their mouths but speed them up so you could just barely understand them. Sometimes you didn't understand them, but at least you got the general idea. Sometimes we would have to slow the track down if we felt it necessary to understand a particular word or sentence.

We gave them both the same personality, but something was missing. Bill Peet came up with the suggestion of making one of them a little goofball to give them two different personalities. Immediately, I saw the advantage of that and took the suggestion. We were trying to name them, and we all sat around with blank stares on our faces. Suddenly, Bee Selck, my assistant director at the time, mentioned chipendale. Immediately, the name clicked with me as a take-off on the furniture called Chippendale and on the word "chip" from chipmunks. I said, "That's it!" It was just a perfect name for the two of them. They went on to become famous, not only as foils for the Duck, but as strong personalities who were able to work alone. They counteracted the Duck's personality. They were industrious little guys and they'd be storing nuts for the winter or something, and the Duck would come across the situation and see a chance to have a little fun. Naturally, it always backfired on him,and then his ill temper would come along and [this] gave us a natural story point.

JK: Who did the voices for Chip 'n' Dale?

A secretary in one of the business offices, Dessie Flynn, who is now Dessie Flynn Miller, and a girl from Ink and Paint were the original ones. She had quite a giggle. I'd act like a monkey and she'd giggle like crazy. We stuck with those two ladies for most of the time. Although we would occasionally use other female voices for the character.

JK: You also developed Humphrey the Bear as another foil?

For the sake of something new, we tried the Duck with a bear in *Rugged Bear* and it seemed like an immediate success for them to play against each other. At the time we had not named the bear. Later, when we started thinking of another picture for the bear, it seemed natural to be in a national forest, and that's how the Little Ranger came into being. We again used the bear, and now he got the name Humphrey. The Little Ranger's voice was done by Bill Thompson, who did several voices in the different shorts, as well as doing the voice for the White Rabbit in *Alice*. One of the sequences I remember having a lot of fun with was when the Duck had a honey farm next to the Ranger's station. The Duck complained that the bears were stealing the honey, so the Little Ranger had them stand up in a police line-up fashion. The Little Ranger always treated his bears like his own pets. Sometimes I would fill in and do some of Humphrey's grunts.

JK: You also had Donald battling a lot of bees in your pictures.

I don't recall any real reason for that. Probably the idea was that the bee is a menace with that stinger as a weapon and is much smaller than the Duck, so it would be funny having the little guy battling a big bully. You can get a funny sound effect out of a bee. They can cuss you out with that little bee noise. I know we did go to smaller characters with the Duck because it would make it funnier when the situation backfired on him. Just having Donald and his nephews made it difficult to come up with story ideas after a while. We considered the nephews just the same character. We never really considered them individuals. They each acted the same; as far as we were concerned, they were interchangeable. You couldn't use much dialogue with them and the Duck because you wouldn't be able to understand it.

JK: So was it difficult directing Clarence Nash as the voice of Donald Duck?

Clarence was always nice to work with. He did many little side voices, such as meowing cats or miscellaneous characters. One problem we always had was the understanding of Duck lines. He was great when he lost his temper and all of that. However, we had to pantomime pretty well in the drawing what the Duck was thinking or doing because if you tried to get over a gag or a line of dialog with understanding, you were in trouble using that voice. We had the same problem with the nephews because Clarence would use the same voice only at a higher pitch. I know when we'd take the Duck through some of those tantrums that Nash would get red in the face and darn near pass out. That's one thing I'll say about Clarence Nash: he was a hard worker, and I actually thought a couple of times he was going to faint on me. The blood would come to his face on these wild tantrums, especially when they were prolonged.

I did notice over a period of time a change in Clarence's voice as he got older. His voice became a little more guttural and a little less understandable. In fact, I've gone back and heard many of the earlier films like *Band Concert*, where the voice was much more understandable when he was a younger man. Even though he used the same method of getting that voice, he seemed much more understandable when he was younger. His voice has gotten very guttural, and it's almost impossible to understand the lines. That happens to all of us.

JK: So the biggest problem was getting Donald Duck to be understood?

It was the bane of my existence! That voice! Getting anyone to understand the Duck! It was aggravating as hell to do a picture with dialogue and not be able to understand the main character. But he did have a variety of moods and you could get over with strong poses what he was trying to tell you. I got some old acetates of a television show I made, and I notice that Jimmie Dodd says, "And now, Donald, we're going to take you around the world." The Duck asks, "Around the world?" Jimmie replies, "Yes, that's right. Around the world." We did it that way to be damn sure you could understand what was being said. Once a human said it, then you could understand the way the Duck said it. We did that in some of the cartoons as well. If you heard the line repeated by a straight voice, it made it easier to understand the Duck.

We always did a minus-dialogue track whenever we did a cartoon so they could do foreign voices and fill them in for foreign release. Jack Cutting was in charge of the foreign department and he made sure the foreign voices were done, and I never had anything to do with any of that. Well, not long ago, I talked with Clarence Nash on the phone. I mentioned something like, "Well, on those foreign voices, that was one good thing. You didn't have to redo the Duck in different languages." But Clarence was very proud of the fact that anybody could understand him doing the Duck and he replied, "Oh, yes, I do Spanish. Listen to this." And he did it in Spanish over the phone and he did a couple of other languages, and to me it still sounded like the same old English you couldn't understand. But Clarence, knowing what he was supposed to be saying, naturally thought everyone else could understand him.

JK: Under your direction, Donald certainly became more defined and I think it is your version that most people think of when they think of Donald Duck in animation.

I worked in a minor role on several of Donald's very early films. One in particular was *The Band Concert*. I had a little to do with the real early stages of his development. As I remember, he was drawn with a pointed beak and gangling arms and legs. By the time I got into close contact with him, his anatomy had changed gradually into rounder, cuter shapes. I'm not sure some of his "character" was lost in the drawing change. Of course, every artist drew every character slightly different, even with "model sheets" which were made in an attempt to avoid this. Animator Fred Spencer had a lot to do with the change-over of Donald's drawing style. Then, through the years, animators or directors tried different styles. Some drew him more stylized, almost toward abstract. The comic-strip department even had their idea of how he should look and I definitely argued with their version. But, as I said, there were always bound to be differences. I knew every animator, and I could damn near tell even if I hadn't handed out the scenes, almost every animator that worked on my picture. Animation is that distinctive, and yet probably the average person couldn't tell the difference. It was hard—even sitting there and saying "You have to make the beak longer or shorter or whatever." You were bound to get those differences. That's one of the big problems of animation: keeping the animators drawing the character the same. Some of them drew him with a bigger head, some more pear-shaped. The thing was to insure that at least your viewing audience didn't notice that.

JK: It wasn't just Donald's physical appearance. I think you helped refine his personality as well. For instance, you eliminated his "angry arm pumping."

It had outlived its humor as far as most of us were concerned. I got tired of putting Donald through tantrum attacks for no reason. I think an animator first created that bit where he has one arm outstretched and he hops up and down.

JK: How would you describe Donald Duck?

I would describe Donald as a lovable twerp who never could stay out of trouble—and he usually brought it on himself. For instance, if he came across a bee gathering honey, Donald would slyly place an obstacle in the bee's path and enjoy the bee's discomfort. It would seem to sometimes make Donald cruel, but his prank would always backfire. I always considered him a comic villain. Of course, when his trick turned on him, he would lose his famous temper. I think everyone sees comedy in an uncontrolled temper. He was a comic villain. That's probably the best way to describe him. He was villainous but in a mild way. He just wanted to get the best of somebody or something, but he never did. He was a forgivable villain because the other guy always won out. Donald's motive was never really vicious; he just let his temper run away with him. He still lives, even though he hasn't appeared in a short for quite some time. If you asked people, "What three or four cartoon characters come to your mind first?" I think Donald would be on that list. Donald was an accident. Just like in real life, someone comes on as an extra and then BOOM! Most of the popular animated characters were accidents. They just seemed to work for an audience.

JK: *No Hunting* (1955) seems to be a different kind of Donald Duck short.

I recently showed that short to a group of my students at Cal Arts and the reaction was very favorable. Thirty years later the laughs and dull spots still came in the same places. People don't change much. Good basic comedy never seems to change. I used to go hunting with my dad when I was a kid and this short was a great takeoff on these hunters and fishermen. They really are this way. They are as dangerous to themselves as to the game they're hunting. I've heard there are more hunters shot on opening day than deer. It shows how timeless these shorts are because it still spoofs hunters and fishermen. They're still that way. My students especially enjoyed the joke where all the trash cans are coming down the river and I stuck in Bambi's mother, who says, "Man is in the forest. Let's dig out." There was sort of a subtle feeling in the short that Donald wasn't himself, which is why he doesn't talk. Hunting didn't mean a thing to him, but it was the spirit of his grandfather that came out of the painting off the wall that got into him and now made a monster of him. He was possessed. That's why he didn't speak. Donald just wasn't himself. I never thought of that later as being one of my better shorts, but after seeing it recently, I've changed my opinion.

Several times when we needed incidental lines from minor characters, we found talent right within the unit. Milt Schaffer was a storyman at Disney. We used his voice when the usher said, "Two down front," when the hunters were trying to find room for camps. I don't think he got story credit, but I know he did work on that story. Talking about this particular short, I stuck my voice in several times. Remember where the spirit of the Duck had antlers on and a moose was down in a hole with him, and the moose says, "Hmmm, you're a cute one."? That's my voice! The animator I was working with on that sequence, John Sibley, got a big kick out of the way I said it, so I finally said, "Hell, I'll record it." And I did. In several of my shorts, I did those kinds of things. Little one-liners. Grunts for Humphrey the Bear. That sort of thing.

JK: What was it like working on the Donald Duck 3-D cartoon, *Working for Peanuts* (1953)?

That was the rage about then to have 3-D pictures on the screen, so we tried it with Donald working with an elephant and the chipmunks. The main thing I remember about working in 3-D was to be sure there were plenty of effects. The effects had to be designed so that they would come out at you. Anything we could do to take advantage of the third dimension, we used. I was "green" at it and didn't know much about it, so we loaded it with animated effects like water coming right at you. Later, I think they turned around and remade it into a conventional short, too, but I don't think I ever saw it in anything except 3-D.

JK: While you are known as a "Duck Man", you did direct other Disney characters in animated shorts.

I directed Goofy in a couple of shorts. One dealt with basketball, another had the Goof in the jungle, and I also did one where he was a duck hunter. I worked with Art Babbitt on it, and we really had a lot of fun doing it. Art was always a very fine Goof animator. I'd probably say he was one of the better ones, and knew more about the Goof and had more to do with the building of his personality than anyone I can think of. He did a lot of that animation for me. Art and I remained friends despite the problems he may have had at the studio.

I never remember having a preference in terms of the characters I directed. Naturally, I welcomed having a change after directing one character for most of my life. I enjoyed working with the Goof. I loved it when I got a "special" like *Lambert, the Sheepish Lion* because there I was able to work with different personalities. *Lambert* started with Bill Peet, then went to Ralph Wright, and then I picked it up. I had no contact with the story people who had developed it. I did more changing and developing in that story than [in] any other I picked up. I went to the studio to get a print to show at Cal Arts and learned that the last remaining original print was given to the Emperor of Japan by Roy Disney because the Emperor enjoyed it so much. I did two or three shorts with Pluto in [them], and it was kind of fun, again primarily because of the change. I guess I was just known as a Duck Man, so I always seemed to end up with the Duck back in my lap.

JK: There seems to be an inside joke in one of the Goofy shorts you did, *Double Dribble* (1946). The basketball players are named Kinney, Berg, Lounsbery, Hannah, Sibley, etc.

It was done by the storymen as an inside joke. Obviously the audience wouldn't have found it funny, because they didn't know the names were all Disney story men. It was probably done to relieve the boredom of doing a story. By the way, we were thinking of Dick Kinney, who was Jack Kinney's younger brother, and in the Story Department at the time. I really can't recall any more inside jokes offhand. We didn't go out of our way to put them in, but in this story it just seemed to fall into place. I mean, you had to use some names, and "Kinney" was just as good as "Jones" or "Brown". If Walt had had some objection to it, you can bet we would have heard about it, but we didn't. We didn't put ears on the characters, so it would be clear that they were just "Goof" characters and not Goofy himself.

JK: Did you ever use rotoscoping in any of your shorts?

Once. You know the girls in *Dude Duck*? Bill Justice animated those girls using the rotoscope as a guide only. We had a set built and filmed the girls as they left the bus and ran toward the camera. We didn't really need to do it that way, but it gave us a chance to look at girls in sweaters. The problem with rotoscoping is that you're really disappointed if you can recognize it is rotoscoping. A lot of people have had that problem with rotoscoping.

JK: Eight of the cartoons you directed were nominated for Oscars, including one of my favorites, *Trick or Treat* (1952).

I also enjoyed directing *Trick or Treat* because I got a chance to work with a different personality. June Foray, who did such a great job as the voice of the witch, still mentions the film to me whenever I see her. The short got a very high ARI [Audience Reaction] rating when the studio watched it in the sweatbox. Walt said he couldn't understand some of the words, that the dialog was too fast. That reminds me that my dad liked my cartoons, but thought they were too fast as well. Maybe he was just old because now I agree with him. Then I didn't. I heard that Carl Barks later adapted the cartoon into a comic-book story, but I never saw it.

JK: Speaking of Carl, why did you never use the character of Scrooge McDuck in a short?

We did consider Scrooge McDuck for use in a short. I recall vaguely somebody thinking that a character that went wild over money wasn't funny. I remember discussing this with somebody, and we felt that the greed of money seemed to be the reason we didn't use Scrooge. It was at the time that we were also stopping production on the shorts, so that ended any further discussion. Even though he was very funny in comic-book form, we decided he wasn't strong enough at the time. [Editor's note: A short named *Scrooge McDuck and Money* was later released in 1967.]

JK: Did you ever do extensive work on a Donald Duck cartoon that never got finished?

Yes, there was this one Duck short where the Duck was working with some small animal like a baby elephant. It never hit the screen. Strangely enough, it wasn't the Duck's voice this time that caused the problem, but the other character's voice. We had this young guy come in and do the voice and he was just terrible. I should have said, "Sorry, this isn't the voice", but I didn't. I thought we could do something with it in animation. Fergie [Norm Ferguson] was assigned to me to do a lot of the animation. He was having some health problems at the time, so he couldn't do his best work for me. I called Walt and said, "I've got this picture put together. I can't see a thing I can do with it. It would cost more money to fix it up than to junk it right now and start a new one." Walt said, "Well, if it's that bad, I agree with you." Walt knew what was going on, so that's why he didn't say anything else. I just threw it out and never saw it again. That's the only time that ever happened to one of my films after it had gotten along that far.

JK: Did you preview any of your shorts?

Quite often. I remember the old Alex Theatre in the Glendale area was a favorite testing spot. There were two or three other theaters nearby where we'd run a short. We never changed anything after we previewed them for an audience. All the changes had already been made after all the staff previews at the studio. We previewed a short just to get a feel on audience appeal. Audience appeal is so important. I run shorts now for my students and the belly laughs are at the same place and the dead spots are at the same place they were many, many years ago.

JK: How did you get involved directing for the Disney television show?

I started getting wind that the Disney shorts were waning in popularity at the studio because of the cost. They were running us between $90,000 and $100,000 for a seven-minute short, and, as a result, Walt couldn't make his money back for several years. With all the reissues, they've become a gold mine. But at the time, the cost was prohibitive, and a lot of other cartoon studios were finding it too expensive a process and had to stop cartoon production. In the meantime, ABC came along and wanted a television series, so animation got a sort-of rejuvenation because it could be used in the TV series.

I was lucky being a Duck Man because Donald was going to be used quite extensively on the new television program. In fact, we would get the national ratings and such, and they showed the Duck shorts with Walt would get some of the highest ratings. That relieved some of the pressure of the cost of cartoons because it was absorbed in television.

On the first shows, live-action directors were hired to direct the live action, but Walt sensed they couldn't "feel" the presence of unseen animated characters, so Walt had me join the Director's Guild.

One of the big problems we had was that the camera operator couldn't get used to it that there was another actor there, and would frame the picture so it was wrong. Eventually, we had to use a cardboard cutout to make everyone happy. We used an awful lot of the old shorts in [the] making of those shows. We'd tie a couple of the old shorts together with some new material around one theme, and used a lot of old footage in this manner. One show that I worked on that seems to be rerun a great deal is "From All of Us to All of You." Each year, the material has gradually changed to freshen the show so that little of my work remains in the show now.

JK: What was the biggest challenge in doing these shows?

The biggest problem was trying to tell Walt what to do. He already knew what he was going to do. He really seemed to enjoy those parts because he was working with cartoon people rather than with humans. He seemed to feel at home with these characters. Walt was really a very good actor. Anything he ever got into, he wouldn't even try it unless he was going to be one of the best. I remember having a few moments when things got a little bit sticky trying to direct him with a whole crew on the sound stage. Walt was a great one for trying to have a little fun at your expense in front of other people. Generally, it was fine. We had everything worked out carefully ahead of time, and I'm sure he went over the lines very carefully ahead of time because he knew the situation and he didn't stumble around when we got ready to shoot it. The stand-in would come in and we'd get the scene lighted and Walt would come on and worked with an idiot card, a cue card, especially on the longer speeches. However, when he was playing with the Duck, he had it all worked out, even his mannerisms. He knew ahead of time what he wanted to do. Many times in the lighter situations, he would ad-lib with Donald and that would surprise us, and we'd have to go back and revise the storyboard.

JK: What did Disney think of your directing?

I remember after we screened the first television show which I directed, Walt started to walk out, and as he was leaving the room, without even turning his back, said, "Good work, Jack." I still remember that moment very clearly because it's the only compliment I ever remember him giving me while I was in the same room.

JK: After directing fourteen of the television shows, you left the Disney studio.

The studio was going more and more into live action. They had done as much as they could with the Duck at the studio. You can only go so far tying him into stories like showing the Mouseketeers through the studio, and the life of Donald Duck, etc. In the meantime, I had gotten the "live-action bug" and wanted to be a live-action director, and I suggested this to Walt several times. He was not about to take this suggestion from me, and, in fact, we had a few heated discussions on this subject. I was aware I had come to an impasse at Disney's. Gerry Geronimi, who was a long-time friend of Walter Lantz, talked to me. He had gotten wind of my predicament and told Lantz to get in touch with me. He told me he was very short on stories and said, "Bring your first story with you", if I decided to move over there. I got Milt Banta to work with me on the story. I brought Walter the story and he accepted it. I went right to work preparing it. It was called *Freeloading Feline*. It was in 1959 that I went over there, even though my first short wasn't released until 1960.

JK: Did any of your crew at Disney come with you?

When I left Disney, they were breaking up my whole unit. I took Riley Thomson with me, who was a very good draftsman. He worked at Disney for years, did a little direction, a little animation, and, of course, he did comic strips. I took Riley as my layout man when I went over to Lantz's. Yale Gracey, who was my layout man at the time, was transferred over to WED Enterprises. One of my background painters, Ray Huffine, had no place to go, and Lantz said, "Fine. Bring him along." So I took him over to Lantz as well. Al Coe was a good animator who never reached the stature as far as his name was concerned, but he was a real good all-around animator who worked with me at Disney's. He did a lot of the Humphrey the Bear stuff for me. He worked out fine in my unit at Lantz's. Even after I left, the people I brought with me stayed on.

JK: Did you ever see Walt Disney when you were working at Lantz?

Within a few months after I left Disney and was working at Lantz's, we all met at the Masquers Club. It was a dinner for artist Jimmy Swinnerton, sort of a testimonial type thing. I was sitting with the Lantz gang at a big table and Walt Disney was sitting across the room and he evidently spotted me, and he came over and asked Walter how I was doing. He said something like "Is he breaking you like he broke me?" Lantz replied, "Jack just finished his first picture and it's right on budget." Walt didn't say much after that. He got up and left. That was the only direct meeting I had with Walt until I rejoined the studio at a later date.

JK: I know you directed for Lantz, including directing his *Woody Woodpecker* television series, and did some work for Bob Clampett and then left animation. So how did you end up back at Disney?

I had left animation and was getting more involved with my oil painting. My work was being shown in galleries throughout the Western states. In the early sixties, I got a call from the Disney studio and Walt himself invited me back to work on live-action stories as a story consultant. He had been complaining that they hadn't gotten enough cartoon ideas into their live action. These so-called comedy writers were way too straight when writing comedy action. Walt wanted someone to help in this area, and my name came up. I was still teaching painting, but I said I would come in a couple of days a week and still keep my painting classes. They gave me a script, and then I would go through and try to "plus" different situations in the picture. Or maybe take a main sequence and try to develop it further.

I was working with Walt and Jim Algar on a picture called *Rascal* when Walt died. Soon after that, I had to go into the hospital for some surgery, and so I left the studio and didn't go back after that. Other than keeping [in] contact with a few old friends there, I had completely divorced myself from the animation business. One day in 1975, I got a surprise call from out of the blue asking if I would be interested in heading a school of animation at the California Institute of the Arts.

JK: Who called you?

It was Ken Anderson. I asked him why they were calling me and he said, "it's because you are a fighter!" That's funny because at one time I had seriously considered going into professional fighting and had even won a Golden Gloves competition. It wasn't until I broke my jaw during a professional fight that I decided it was better to be an artist. At first, I was speechless, but I finally agreed to come to the studio and have several meetings with some of the old timers who had some ideas about developing a character-animation program.

Walt had this dream of having a school with all the performing arts under one roof. It was a beautiful idea, but before he could see it through he passed on and the school got into some ultra-liberal hands, so Walt's dream never really came true.

Realizing the great opportunity that had been afforded them through their lives, some of the senior animators at the studio wanted to share that art of character animation with new generations. The more I talked with people at the studio, the more the idea sounded inviting, so I accepted. I collected a crew of six instructors who were ex-Disney experts in various areas such as background and layout, and we formed a unit in 1975 and started with about sixteen students. We determined to pass on many of the philosophies of Walt himself, as they still hold true today. Today, we get applications from all around the world. One of my students was John Lasseter. We specialize in animation, but expose the student to as many aspects of fine arts as possible, knowing they need this information to become better animators. I am truly excited by the program. There was such a demand for good animators that studios would pick our students up even after they had finished just two or three years in the program.

JK: What was your impression of Walt Disney?

Everybody always asks, "What did you think about Walt?" I could spend the whole afternoon talking about him. Walt was one of the toughest men to work for. There were times when you might have hated him but you always respected him.

Walt had a great story mind. He knew what would entertain. He really couldn't draw well. He probably couldn't even draw the Mouse's tail very well for that matter, but he was the driving force. Probably the story that best describes Walt was one that took place right before the war and just as Walt was making plans to move the studio. They had these blocks arranged on a table and Walt would move them around, saying things like "The animation building should be here." While he was doing this, somebody asked him, "But, Walt, what about the war?" Walt supposedly was to have answered, "What war?"

I'll never forget one time I was doing a lot of woodworking at home. I was making a big "lazy susan", but the piece of wood I was using was too big for my lathe. So on Saturdays I'd go down to work at the shop at the studio. Walt was also coming in on Saturdays to work in the shop. I had a big sack of cigars and left them on the bench while I went upstairs to use the big lathe. When I came back down, Walt was there working away, and I said, "Well, I've got some cigars there if you want one." And he said, "Thanks, I've already helped myself." He'd gone over and taken one of my cigars and had already smoked it. These were the old ten-centers, the best I could afford at the time. I always got a kick out of that where he just went over and took it without asking or anything. He was that kind of guy. He'd turn right around and be one of the guys on a Saturday, but on Monday morning, if I met him in the hall, maybe he would speak to me and maybe he wouldn't. That's the kind of guy he was.

When the studio first started doing live action, one day I cautiously peeked onto a sound stage where they were doing some filming because I was just fascinated by the whole business and wanted to move into live-action directing. Walt saw me and welcomed me in. Out of curiosity, and to keep the conversation going, I asked who was directing the picture. I can't remember what he said, but we talked for a while and I left. Later on, some friends came to me and said that Walt had been in a story meeting and had mimicked me coming in with a strut and throwing a cigar around and demanding, "Who's directing this picture?" And Walt had said he replied, "A guy named Yensid." (Disney spelled backwards.) I supposedly puffed away on my cigar and said, "Yes. Yes. I know his work. He'll do fine." And they all laughed their heads off. Walt did this to many of the guys. He loved embellishing stories and having fun at somebody else's expense.

But you can't deny that he was a genius. There's no doubt about it. There was an awe about him. You just felt it if he was in the same wing of a building you were in. I know it sounds weird, but you never got over that awe of him. He had a tremendous faith in the future of animation. Things he said back in the thirties, I use in my teaching today. He was a creative man and he took animation about as far as I believe anybody could have in those days. He was always looking for something new. How could he top himself? How could he top *Pinocchio* or *Snow White* or some of those other great old ones?

I believe that's why the Disney parks came about. It was a new adventure for Walt, a new toy to explore. It was the same way when he first started with live-action films. When I went back to the studio as a story consultant on live action, I can honestly say he was spending most of his time on the third floor where most of the writers and directors were working on live action. Toward the end of his life, I do feel that Walt had cooled in his excitement toward animation somewhat. Maybe today, seeing all the new technology that is available for use in animation would have rekindled his interest. Who knows? I don't think anyone ever really knew Walt or what he was going to do or why he was going to do it. That's what made him Walt.

JK: Any closing thoughts about Jack Hannah?

I'm very comfortable now. I have no desire to get back into animation. I enjoy what I'm doing now. I don't feel in competition with these new guys. I just feel good when I see them use the knowledge I give them. Animation is a great teamwork thing. I've worked with so many top pros. So many top pros are gone. It's sort of funny, though. Nobody ever seems old in this business. Basically, I don't think what I think of my work means a hell of a lot; it's what the audience thinks that counts. That's what I try and teach my students.

© 2004 Jim Korkis

John Hench (1908–2004)

Interviewed by Alain Littaye on June 24, 1996

Had John Hench lived just a few more months, he would have celebrated his 65th year working for Disney. Needless to say, it makes it almost impossible to list all of the Disney projects with which John was involved.

John was hired by Disney in May 1939 to work as a sketch artist, and quickly moved to background painting for *Fantasia* and later *Dumbo*. He then joined the layout team on *The Three Caballeros* and *Fun and Fancy Free*; served as art director on *Make Mine Music*; did color and styling for *The Adventures of Ichabod and Mr. Toad, Cinderella, Alice in Wonderland*, and *Peter Pan*; developed the cartoon art treatment for combining live action and animation in *So Dear to My Heart*; created animation effects for *The Living Desert*; made lead title special-effect credits for the Academy Award-winning movie *20,000 Leagues Under the Sea*; worked with Salvador Dali on the animated short project *Destino*; and then moved to WED (now known as Walt Disney Imagineering) in 1954.

While at WED, John was first involved in the creation of Tomorrowland for Disneyland, and then worked, among other projects, on the organization of the 1960 ceremonies for the Winter Olympics and on Disney's contributions to the 1964 World Fair. John also led WED from 1972 to 1982 as Executive Vice President, and remained until 2004 as WDI's "color guru".

In June 1996, Alain Littaye had the pleasure of interviewing John in his office at Walt Disney Imagineering. At the time of the interview, John was choosing the colors to be used for the Magic Kingdom castle during Walt Disney World's 25th anniversary celebration.

[Alain's questions were prepared by Didier Ghez.]

....

Alain Littaye: How did you enter the Walt Disney Company?

John Hench: Well, it happened in 1939. I wanted to be a fine-art painter, and I reached the point in art schools where I needed to understand more about images and how images communicate information to people. And I was not getting very far in that from my professors.

So I thought that it would be easier to learn if I worked in motion pictures. So I went to work with one motion-picture producer who was developing a color system. This didn't do much good to me. All I did was pick out filters for the camera. The other thing I tried was working for special effects, which was not what I was looking for.

So I finally came to Disney, who was hiring people for *Fantasia*. I like classical music, so I thought, "This is fine." And I found what I was after because the studio had developed a great skill in producing images that have great meaning for people.

Mickey is one of the prime examples: Mickey has never been suspected of being an American export. It was déjà vu. They gave him a local name, and he has been accepted everywhere he goes. Even in China. Children there, next to the Great Wall, who had never seen Mickey Mouse, responded. So the studio did have that skill to communicate with images.

Of course, it gave the studio an enormous power because I don't know any other place—at that time—that had that skill to communicate with images. And the need for these kinds of images is even greater now than it ever was because we are losing our life symbols. We don't have too much ritual in our lives anymore. And these life symbols, which people rely on to keep their feeling of well-being, the feeling that life is not too bad after all, are required more and more....

AL: You went through a record number of different jobs while you worked at Disney. Which one did you enjoy the most?

I enjoyed all of them! I still enjoy all of them! But I was curious about how did it work, how did it function? And so I went from one job to another....

Even to the Camera Department. One day, I told Walt: "I would like to work on Camera for a while." He said "Well, really? What for?" And I explained to him that some of the scenes—I was in background painting then—didn't come out right. And I thought they had lit them wrong, particularly on the multiplane camera. So Walt said "Fine," and I stayed there for three years.

And I helped develop Disney's special-effects department at that time, which helped very much when we worked on *20,000 Leagues Under the Sea*.

Then I started to work on Disneyland, on the idea of a theme park. Walt said one day when he walked by my desk "I want you to work on Disneyland...and you are going to like it!" And he kept on going. I didn't even have a chance to answer!

But I did like it. Because it was much the same kind of things achieved in the movies but in another way, a three-dimensional way. We have the long shot when you're coming in, then people come to the close-ups. When you're going from Main Street to Adventureland, there is a threshold. The painting is different, you get information from your feet that you are crossing something, and the music is different, etc. Walt put everything he knew about communication with images into the park, so it was very familiar.

AL: When I am trying to explain to people in France who have never been in the park, I always tell them that Disneyland is a kind of accomplishment of the love of men for illusion. After the magicians in the ancient times, the modern magic from Robert Houdin, then came the cinema, and finally the theme park concept. Which is a kind of three-dimensional illusion....

That's right. And it achieved a kind of reality. Like these virtual reality games the children are playing. I told them we were doing this 40 years ago! Disneyland is virtual reality....

Walt had a marvelous intuition. Because he understood people very well, liked them, and had great respect for people, there was nothing cynical about Walt. In other studios I worked for, they were all cynical! When they did bad pictures, they were saying: "They won't know the difference!" But it's wrong; people do see the difference, and it's because they have feelings. They don't see it from the intellect, but from feelings.

And Walt understood all of those things, and even common things about people. For instance: usually you get your idea of what kind of day it is by looking at the horizon because the horizon is at the eye level. So what Walt did is to eliminate the horizon. When you go to the park, there is no horizon—just Disneyland.

And so the environment is very special because nothing leaks in from outside. Even the sun is brighter! You have an impression of better weather inside the park than you do outside.

You know, since we're born, the first thing we fight for in life is that feeling of being alive—and it's the last thing, too. We never want to give up that experience of being alive. And this is the secret of Disneyland: everywhere in the park, it's like a pat in the back telling you: "You're okay. Life is good."

We've achieved this feeling, for instance, with the colors. The colors in the park are harmonious with each other, not like in big cities. Big cities are chaotic. And chaos for humans—who have experience from their ancestors—is the last step before conflict. So, in the park, every kind of visual contradiction has been eliminated.

We were trained from our work with cartoons. Everything that was on the screen was chosen. Anything that was not there was deliberately not there. In live-action movies, you just hope that everything works. Because the actor may have had a bad morning and doesn't act well, or accidents happen continuously. Many things contradict what you are trying to say. But in cartoons, nothing contradicts what you want to say. And I think that's why Walt got into cartoons because he knew he would have control. A director doesn't have much control, really. Only a little. Except maybe some great directors like Stanley Kubrick or David Lean.

AL: Talking about movies: You told me before that you worked on *20,000 Leagues Under the Sea*. What kind of special effects were you involved in?

Well, there were a lot of special effects in that film as you know. I did what we call "dry for wet" effects, some of the miniature work, and two animation sequences.

I even took the place of the actor who played Professor Aronnax, in the scene where Professor Aronnax is sitting in his cabin, making an entry in his diary about a storm overhead on the surface. We could not find Paul Lukas that day. So I put on a coat and played his role. Actually, it's my hand that you see writing on the diary. Not in Spencerian script, because I didn't have time to practice. You'll see it in the movie.

AL: There is this famous never-finished animated project called *Destino*, on which you worked....

Oh, *Destino*! Yes, it was with Salvador Dali. The theme of *Destino* was about space, time, and love. It was supposed to be 10-12 minutes long, and would have been included in what they called at that time a package picture. But at that time, suddenly our distributor, RKO, didn't want any more of these package pictures, and Walt reluctantly suspended production of the short.

So there is only the story plus a short test that I did. Because I thought that, when Walt would see images on the screen, he might want to go ahead with production. I shot a test with Dali. It was supposed to be animated, but there were no animators available for me at the time! So we did something which was more animation effects than real animation.

But the story was complete as were the storyboards, too. And even the plans for production. Walt was sorry afterwards. He said we should have gone ahead and made it anyway. Because of the value of the document.

But working with Dali was wonderful. We shared the same sense of irrationality. He came every day to the studio for about a year. There were breaks in between, of course, where he went back to his home in Spain. I went up there. We were good friends, and we worked on many other things later. I helped him for the *Leda and the Swan* painting [Editor's note: the painting is actually called *Leda Atómica*], for instance. He was not good at perspective of shadows. I helped him on several canvases....

AL: What was the origin of the project?

Dali was working for Warner Brothers on the Hitchcock movie *Spellbound*, and he stayed at Jack Warner's house in Beverly Hills. Walt met him at dinner because Jack Warner and Walt were friends. Walt asked him if Salvador would like to come over and do something for us. Dali said "Yes." And so he came to the studio.

We had a piece of music, and Walt said, "Why don't we make an animated short out of this?" And that's how it happened. The music was very banal, but Dali didn't mind because he knew he could get a handle on anything. He could take the banality out of anything!

The fact is that Salvador enjoyed banal things, really. He was crazy about the worst western pictures in the world. He would reinvent the whole story: from the stampede and the longhorn cattle, he would tell you that, in fact, it was all about the libido of one of the actors!

So he was never bored by anything because he re-interpreted. One of the things he would be doing was taking the dictionary and making a Dali equivalent for every word. He reinterpreted each word in a "Dalinian" manner and gave it a new meaning! This is tremendous work!

He and Walt shared the same kind of optimism. Walt believed in himself, and he was optimistic about what he wanted to do. He just knew it would be okay, and Dali was the same way. They had a great deal in common that way.

AL: Can you tell us about the Disneyland attractions projects you worked on that were never built?

Well, nothing really important. Nearly all of them were built. Of course, there is this Chinese restaurant project with a golden dragon and Confucius to entertain guests. Both of them were Audio-Animatronics, and Confucius was there to answer wisely to questions. It was supposed to be in the second street project for Main Street. But who knows? Maybe it will be built one of these days. We never throw away any idea....

For instance, some early ideas for Florida were done only recently. The idea of a little village was there from the beginning and now we have this "Celebration" village. Same thing for the Disney Institute. Walt talked about that idea right from the start.

Some other ideas changed from the initial concept. The Tiki Room, for instance, was supposed to be a Polynesian restaurant. I had even ordered the tables, I had bought all the furniture. And Walt was listening one morning to a rehearsal of the show, and he said: "If we get rid of the tables, how many more people can we get in here?" So I took the tables out, arranged the chairs in a certain way, etc. And he said:

"That's what we're gonna do. I'll handle the man who was to operate the restaurant. So we can make a show out of it."

The Enchanted Tiki Room show was all ready but didn't had a curtain riser. It didn't have a start, as it was originally supposed to start up very gradually. Walt's idea was that, as soon as the people who were dining got through their main course and got to their dessert, something would happen: a bird would start to do a little jazz thing on this music that was supposed to only come from tapes like in any restaurant. And then another bird would start to answer him, and people would say: "Something is going on here! What is this?",and the show would have come to life very gradually....

But, with no restaurant, you can't make a show like that. It must have an overture. And we tried to fix that right up until the last minute before The Tiki Room's official opening.

We had to pretend that the birds were asleep. Somebody came in saying, "Hey, wake up, wake up!" And we started the show that way which was very bad. I was always embarrassed about this. Because you can't design a show for one operation and then make a change so radically.

Not to mention this Offenbach music in the middle. Which is incredibly boring! I remember that I protested. I'm not a musician myself. But we had a big fight, the composer who did the music and me. His name was Buddy Baker. I'll never forget him!

AL: Do you have memories about the original Epcot project?

I worked on the concept, the first layouts and designs for the property. I remember that—at the beginning—we had two separate models for Future World and World Showcase. And Marty Sklar pushed them together, and we combined them.

I don't think that was too successful. Because I always thought that the two of them should have been more separate. Also I had planned the monorail station to be in the center. So that one day you would have had to go to World Showcase and then the other day to Future World. And I still think that would have been better.

AL: What were your most difficult challenges during your work on Walt Disney World?

I remember Space Mountain: it took us ten years before we found the technology that would allow such a ride. And during these ten years, I had a model that I kept, waiting for the technology we needed.

And one day, we finally found out the technique of separating and getting information about where every train [would be] at any moment.

Of course, it went over budget many times because as it went along, some things improved and we got better ideas.

When we started a project, all my focus was on it, night and day. You never forget it until it's done. I suppose I always had a passionate relation with the projects. Because, you know, it's never hard work when you enjoy yourself. Look, I've been here for 57 years, and I don't have to explain why I've stayed so long. I always enjoyed it.

AL: What is your favorite achievement on Walt Disney World?

Usually, it's the last thing I've worked on. Now, I worked on colors. Color is a very critical thing. I've found that architects don't like colors. Neither do engineers. And so somebody has to stand in. Because it is the emotional part of a structure. I had great satisfaction in doing that.

AL: Sam McKim was a specialist of Western theming, Marc Davis was famous for the humor he introduced in the attractions. What was your specialty?

Well, I suppose that I was a kind of consultant for taste. Is it good taste? Or bad taste? I had an attention to detail, to what would best tell the story. Because many people get excited about the work and drift off from the story.

Like Pirates of the Caribbean, for instance. When you get in, you see on the door: Pirates of the Caribbean. So you expect to see pirates. Then you get on the boat, so you think: "This is okay. We're going to see pirates." The boat goes out and the first scene that you see is the restaurant. So people think: "Hey, these are not pirates. These are people having lunch. What happen to the pirates we are supposed to see?" Then we go down the chutes , and it's where the pirates were. But they're all gone. There is nothing but skeletons down here!

Well, it was never supposed to be like that. Walt died before we had finished it. The original idea of Walt was that you came down there, into the caves, and there were no pirates. But they had been there just seconds before! There was a hot meal on the table, steaming. There was no jewelry. Walt wanted this atmosphere: they were supposed to live here, they've gone outside somewhere, but they could come back at any minute and catch us....

Then you were supposed to discover the city, where they were. But because somebody liked skeletons and discovered that they were available at a cheap price, we used too many skeletons all over the place, and the public got the wrong message. Now people didn't know what it was and what was going on.

AL: In the Paris version, they put the skeletons at the end, not at the beginning.

Well, at least they've learned something!

AL: Have you been to Disneyland Paris?

Yes, and I like it. I chose the colors there to paint the first hotel, the Disneyland Hotel. Because of the cloudy sky we had in Paris, it had to be a particular kind of color to fight those grey days. And also something you can see when you're driving up: "There it is! We're arriving! " And I think it works well.

AL: You knew Ray Bradbury who helped the Imagineers on the Orbitron concept. How was your relationship with him?

Ray is a good friend. And he was a good friend of Walt's, too. We worked on several things for the World's Fair together, on some of the exhibitions for industrial companies, and we're still consulting him occasionally. In fact, I think the studio is working on a cartoon picture from one of his books. He has talked with Roy Disney about it. But I don't know where the project is at this point.

AL: What are you currently doing at WDI?

Well, I happen to be working on two hotels. One is being rehabbed, repainted. And the other one is a large one. Nineteen hundred rooms, themed on the Southwest of the United States. New Mexico, kind of. It's an enormous amount of work: there are 28 separate buildings, and I work on the color choices for everything. Outside colors, balcony colors, etc. And all of this has to work together, in harmony. I also work on the WDW castle. We are going to make a big cake out of it for the 25th anniversary. The logistics of that are just enormous.

AL: What is your fondest memory of Walt?

I always admired his optimism. He seemed to know the direction he was going. When I was at the studio, I remember he kept driving all of us back down to a more fundamental level all the time. When we tried to use, let's say, an event that was current, he said: "No, don't use that! It's all right for now. But I want these pictures to come back for years and I want them to have a meaning. If you use that now, it will be okay for today. But five or ten years from now, what will it mean?" And he was right: we can still release a 40-year-old picture, and it's still good because it still has meaning.

Another memory I have is when I was working on a Stravinsky animation adaptation. It was supposed to be a ballet, and I didn't like it.

Walt said "Why?" And I told him that I didn't know anything about ballet. And he said "Oh...well, here is what I want you to do."

And Walt called the impresario of the Ballet Russe de Monte Carlo. And he arranged for me to go sit backstage for the whole season! For all the performances! And I made a thousand drawings, went back, and did my job without any complaint.

Walt often did these kinds of things. Like letting me go to work down in the Camera Department. Who does this now? Nobody! You have a job, and you stay on it all your life now. Nobody is going from one department to another. Only Walt did that.

I was very fond of him, really...

John Hench (1908–2004)

Interviewed by Didier Ghez on May 20, 1999

The *Destino* project was initiated in 1946 when Disney, who owned the rights to the Mexican love ballad by the same title, asked Salvador Dali to do a story treatment based on his interpretation of the song.

John Hench was appointed to help Dali prepare the storyboards and keep the project coherent. Interestingly, a few years after the project was canceled, the storyboard sketches disappeared in a theft (most of them were recovered afterwards by the studio) and were eventually purchased by an art dealer in New York who asked Dali to autograph them. The dealer had not been able to differentiate between Dali's work and Hench's, and many of the latter's work was authenticated as the work of the master.

Didier Ghez met John Hench while doing research for the book *Disneyland Paris: From Sketch to Reality*. Didier, who had always been fascinated by the project *Destino*, used the opportunity of that encounter to clarify John's working relationship with Dali in the 1940s.

Didier Ghez: What was the story of *Destino*?

John Hench: It was a story about Destiny, of course, and about human relations. Dali was interested in imagery and the fact that an image has a message. He was interested in the fact that the metamorphosis of the image suggested another image behind the first image, and then another one behind that, and so on, without any distortion. This fascinated him. He created many paintings like this. I remember one particularly well: you look at it and it is a landscape. When you continue to look at it, with no distortion, with no movement on the part of the painting, it became…an animal, a golden retriever! You looked at it further and it became a bowl of fruit! This kind of thing fascinated him a great deal.

At some point the female protagonist of *Destino*, who was a dancer, was on an empty plane with just the sky and a bowl. Then two turtles with stretchers on their backs came in, met in the middle of this plane, and the negative space in there became the female protagonist. She would step down and get into the next act. It was full of things of this nature.

DG: Can you tell me how Walt felt about Dali's ideas for that short? Didn't he feel that those ideas were too intellectual or too weird?

No, because they were emotional ideas. It was mainly about love, the extraordinary evolution of images, how they changed from one thing to the other. It is a common experience in life how the meaning of an image will change and become something with a different message.

DG: Did Walt ever comment on *Destino*?

He visited us, and I had shot a little test because I thought it would be fascinating. It was a test with those two turtles. I did not have any animation, but I moved the cels under the camera and I made a female figure that fit, painted it, and dissolved it in the empty space between the two turtles. It was a short scene, but it was also very startling. I thought it would incite him to continue it. That was the only thing that ever got shot. It was around 50 seconds or something like that.

DG: Do you remember any interesting anecdotes related to working with Dali?

It was fascinating. We did all sort of things! I like Dali. He was finishing the *Leda* [*Atómica*] painting and everything in that painting was floating. So I made a design of where the shadows would fall and how the shadows would appear in perspective. He didn't want to use lead to trace the thing. You normally used a piece of paper, you coat the back of the paper with a lead pencil, and then you transferred your drawing and that lead would come out of this paper onto the canvas. He did not want to do that. I said, "Well, we can take a big piece of plastic and *cut* the line and then you can fill it with paint and then you would press it down, take a heavy object and press on it, and it will transfer the paint." He said, "Great." So we did that. It was the first painting he had where we transferred the drawing in actual pigments. That delighted him.

At that time, in Carmel where we were, there was no plastic available. So I boiled a [cup] of sugar, put watercolor in it so it was a little blue-green, and poured it on some marble in a wave pattern. When it got cold and hard, we picked it up and we propped it up, and it cast a shadow and looked fine. He painted it for three days before it go so sticky and full of mustache hairs and things....

And then we invented [many other things]. We had a little plaster cast of Nero, and he wanted to take the nose off and mount it away from the thing so it would cast shadows. I took the nose off, but then I strung it on a little thin almost invisible cord, to support the nose. To our astonishment, on a wet day the nose would turn, and on a dry day it would go back. It was a weather indictor. Nero had become a projector of the weather!

I helped with the jewelry that he designed for Van Cleef and Arpels.

I also made a huge kaleidoscope: that one was really big and there were insects in it. It was a scene out of hell! You did not have to move it for it to perform. There was a baby salamander and insects of this sort. Extraordinary things.

I also made a drawing of a telephone based on the Rafael painting of Saint George and the Dragon. It was an extraordinary telephone: one hoof of the white horse of Saint George was the transmitter and the other hoof the receiver. The base of the telephone itself was the dragon with its scales a marvelous bronze color. Dali was delighted by the drawing of this telephone and wanted to build it right away. After about 20 minutes I heard him say, "No, we can't do it, we have to give it up." I said, "Why? It's feasible." He answered, "It's impossible for anybody on earth to be good enough to talk to on this phone. Not even the Pope himself is [important] enough to talk to through this phone!"

DG: Did Dali actually physically work at the Disney studio at the time?

Yes, he did, and he was driven over every day by Jack Warner's men. He had some friends who visited him at the studio from time to time. For example, there was a famous mathematician called Ghyka, as well as the impresario from the Ballet Russe de Monte Carlo, who would come and see him. But we were busy all the time. In parallel to *Destino*, we worked on some other small projects like the jewelry and some of his problems with his paintings.

During the weekends, he would go to Carmel where he had a studio. And there are other things I would do on my own for him. I brought him an easel which is still in his house.

Then he wanted a swan for the *Leda* [*Atómica*] painting. He said: "Would it be possible for you to find me a swan?" I said I would try. I called a taxidermist who told me "Swans are hard to get. But let me see what I can do. I know a guy in Ontario who has swans." Dali wanted a big swan, a male swan. A week later the taxidermist called me and said, "I have a swan. I have it here now, and I would like you to come down right away and we will go over the pose again."

What I had not told the taxidermist was that, beside the swam, Dali had also requested a very big black rat that would also be stuffed and would be included inside the swan. I asked Dali, "Why is that? Why do you want a black rat?" He said: "If I know that there is a black rat inside, then the feathers of the swan will look more radiant and much whiter."

So I went to the taxidermist to see the swan. When I arrived, I saw that the taxidermist had been injured. He had a cut on his head and some bruises on his body. He took me in there and here was the swan, smelling badly of poultry and fish, a terrible smell. We went over the pose again, with some drawings that I had. He was so beat up and irritated that I was afraid if I told him about the black rat, he would give the whole thing up, thinking he was working for a crazy person. So I did not mention it, thinking: "Dali will never know that there is no black rat in there. It's all psychological any way. And he did, in fact, assume it was there."

It took five days for the thing to be ready. During that time, I talked about the swan at the studio, and one of the guys brought me a newspaper clipping that mentioned that someone had stolen a swan out of West Lake Park. It was city property! Which explained where the swan came from and why the taxidermist was so beat up: a male swan is a very powerful creature; it's a dangerous animal to be around. I brought it to Dali in my convertible at 3 o'clock in the morning because I was afraid of someone stopping me and finding that swan and connecting it with the newspaper story.

When Dali saw the swan he embraced it and exclaimed: "It's possible to love this thing!" And he did love it. He took it back with him to Spain.

Marc Davis (1913–2000)

Interviewed by John Province in 1991 and 1992

It's very difficult to imagine how drastically different Disney animation would have been without Marc Davis. As one of Walt Disney's four surviving "Nine Old Men" responsible for carrying the artistic brunt of the animated feature films, Davis was shrouded by the studio's policy of near (or total) anonymity for employees. But once Davis' accomplishments are revealed, his contributions seem ubiquitous in both the films and the theme parks. As a trusted Disney lieutenant, Davis' 34-year career provided the studio with three different sets of talents embodied in one man: his gifts as an animator and director, an expert story man, and his sense of character design.

Davis signed on at Disney in 1935 and was chosen to assist the already legendary Myron "Grim" Natwick (creator of Betty Boop) to animate the character of Snow White—a plum assignment for the novice Davis. Realistically drawn human characters were far from routine studio fare and were light-years beyond the capabilities of most of the era's animators. "Marc was an expert animator even at that young age," Natwick said to John Province during his last formal interview, conducted shortly before his death in 1992. "I think they had him pegged as an up-and-coming talent even then." After the success of *Snow White*, Davis was given story and character-development work for *Bambi* and quickly become one of a very small group of exceptionally talented artists whom Disney trusted with the studio's crown jewels: the feature films.

Though the Disney studio was rife with budding talent, it was impressed with Davis' character work for *Bambi*, and Walt Disney brass handed down the edict that Davis was to receive intensive animation training under the tutelage of future fellow "Old Man" Frank Thomas—a rare case of an animator's grooming coming at the boss' direct order. As a result, the Davis magic graced most of the feature films then (and now) hailed as classics, and Davis himself is personally responsible for some of the studio's most recognizable characters and finest moments, including some that Walt Disney himself cited as personal favorites. Davis' versatility in characterization seemed absent of limitations. Everything he did, he did well, from the cuddly Flower to the coolly patrician Maleficent, from the wild and angular Cruella De Vil to the shapely sprite Tinker Bell. These characters came to Davis' animation table as flat sketches and left as fully realized characters with distinct personalities that are today globally recognized. Indeed, Davis' realization of Tinkerbell becoming Mickey Mouse's rival as a virtual symbol of the Disney empire.

Davis left Disney's animation department after completing work on *101 Dalmatians*, transferring to WED (known today as Walt Disney Imagineering) where his talents were used to further Disney's interest in Audio-Animatronics attractions for the 1964 World's Fair, and later for the parks in Anaheim and Orlando. Once again, Davis' mastery of characterization, staging, and movement was harnessed to design and supervise the development of Great Moments With Mr. Lincoln, The Haunted Mansion, Pirates of the Caribbean, It's a Small World, America Sings, and the Country Bear Jamboree.

Davis retired in 1978, but continued well into his 80s to be the soft-spoken yet intensely driven artisan that made him such a valuable asset to the Disney organization for decades. His influence was still directly felt as he advised a new class of Disney artists, and his retirement has been far from idle. His studio in Los Angeles was awash with projects in development, including a fully illustrated instructional volume on animal anatomy and movement, and an illustrated treatise on the tribal inhabitants and folklore of Papua-New Guinea, a long-standing interest of Davis'.

This interview is a marriage of two sessions from 1991 and 1992, the latter session conducted mere days after Davis' return from another appearance on behalf of the Disney organization. While his wife (and former student), Alice, prepared a sumptuous lunch, John and Marc repaired to his downstairs studio to undertake the impossible task of capturing a life on tape. As the session unfolded, it became obvious that Davis' Disney career is but one facet of this remarkable man—not merely a great animator, he is a fine artist, an authority on anatomy and movement, a world traveler, a gourmet, an opera buff, and a teacher who used animation as his instructional tool.

John Province: Let's start with your childhood interests—were you a comic strip or cartoon buff?

Marc Davis: When I was a kid, my family moved around a lot, and I lived and grew up in a lot of wild places. I lived in boom towns and oil fields and the like. My father was something of a rainbow chaser. My schooling would be three months here and six months there. Before I got through high school, I had attended 22 different schools. In the time before I was well acquainted with the latest school, I would amuse myself by drawing and found that I was pretty good at it. Then I found I could attract a lot of attention to myself by drawing. [Laughter] Most of the schools I went to didn't have a school newspaper or yearbook. When they did, however, I invariably wound up doing the drawing for it. I came from a family that had a lot of talent, so it wasn't too difficult. That was the beginning, really.

JP: How about formal art training?

The first professional training I received of any kind was when I was 14 years old and we were in Kansas City, Missouri. I attended the Kansas City Art Institute for one summer. There I met others who were interested in art and cartooning. I took a very useful course they used to call "cast", which is where they set up old plaster statues of Greek sculptures and you would then render them very carefully. In the early 1930s, I attended the Otis Art Institute and the California Institute of Fine Art in San Francisco, and a while at Chouinard's here in Los Angeles. Later, I taught an advanced drawing class at Chouinard's one night a week for 17 years.

JP: Do you recall your first contact with Disney animation?

My father had died, and I was thrown into cold reality and had to make a living. I was in Yuba City, California, making advertising posters, stationery, and the like for a small firm. One day the owner of the local movie theater called me and said he had something he thought I should see. It was a Walt Disney cartoon called *Who Killed Cock Robin?*, and I remember being very impressed with it. Some time earlier in Sacramento, I recalled seeing *The Three Little Pigs*. My father was very impressed with it and wanted me to see it. Though we didn't have much money, he found out when it would be playing and arranged for us to go in and just see that, which was a great extravagance at the time.

I recently saw the man I worked for before I came to the studio. He was in the theatrical poster business and became very successful. Occasionally, he comes down or sends me some great thing and thinks I'm the greatest genius who ever was. [Laughter] He is a very, very kind guy.

JP: Was it seeing these shorts that made you decide to apply at the studio?

I would see the Disney cartoons whenever I went to the theater because they were just program fillers at the time. I decided to take a chance and come down to Los Angeles. I had a few contacts in the Los Angeles area and a sort of half-promise of a job at the *Hollywood Citizen*, which no longer exists. I hadn't been here too long when someone said, "You know, Walt Disney is hiring artists—why don't you go see them?" So I did and was accepted immediately.

JP: Did you take the usual entry route as an in-betweener?

The way you began was through a life class the studio had, taught by a man named Don Graham, a marvelous instructor from Chouinard's. For the first two weeks, you were on trial. At the end of that time, if you could draw to Don Graham's satisfaction, you were enrolled in an in-betweening program. You would draw for half a day, and then attend art classes and lectures as a way of paying your way, so to speak. There was an entire building devoted to that kind of thing, and people were in and out of there like a revolving door. They would look over your work and someone would say, "Mr. Jones, Mr. Drake wants to see you." Then he'd pick up his coat and leave. Everybody knew what it meant. We would never see "Jones" again.

JP: Did you go from in-betweening directly into working on *Snow White*?

Yes, the first job I had at the studio was *Snow White*. I don't particularly like the term, but I got stuck with the human characters. They just didn't have that many people who could draw humans. It wasn't a problem for me drawing humans, although I had originally come to the studio with the idea that what I had to offer them was my knowledge in the drawing of animals. When I was in San Francisco and had run out of money for art school, I used to get up early and take the trolley out to Fleishhacker's Zoo. I'd met the man who was the superintendent, and they let me in early so I could follow the keepers. They would take these monsters out of their cages so I could see them well enough to draw them. I had a lot of very interesting experiences with that. [Laughter] One of the things Milt Kahl and I suffered from was that we could both draw so much better than some of the others. We both had a better understanding of the human figure, and there simply weren't that many people who could handle them. After a while, these things just became automatic: "OK, Milt does the Godmother and Marc does the Princess." We both really wanted the opportunity to do some of the things we would have loved to have done and were quite capable of doing.

JP: You worked and trained on *Snow White* under Grim Natwick ?

Yes, I worked with Grim as his assistant on *Snow White*. He was a wonderful guy and a very generous man and a very unique talent. He had studied in Europe with several top artists. He was very excited about anyone he thought was good, such as Bill Tytla and Freddie Moore. Grim thought their stuff very exciting. We used to go through their trash at night after work and I still have a lot of those old rough drawings. [Laughter] I talked to him about a month ago. He's 99 years old and he'll be 100 in August, and he's witty, he's entertaining and bright, and just one marvelous human being.

JP: Do you recall the scenes you worked on in *Snow White*?

I worked on all of Grim's scenes, all of his animation. They threw the assistants kind of a crumb. I do have a dance scene with my name on it. John Culhane, the animation historian, looked it up on the old exposure sheets. I did the model sheets for Snow White in her ragged costume wearing Dutch wooden shoes. I suppose that would really be the first thing I can take any credit for.

JP: You still have a small clay bust you sculpted of Snow White while you were working on the film. Was this something you did on your own or as part of a course of study?

I did it on my own. I wanted to get a conception of how this character looked in three dimensions. There is something I feel when I animate; you can never really understand the character you're animating unless you've had the opportunity to turn it around. Once you've done that, you know it is a three-dimensional object. A lot of the Saturday morning cartoons are like that today, just flat little cut-outs. They're really just designs and not characters at all. Not that there's anything wrong with that, but it is a little different than the problems we were faced with. At the old studio, every day someone did something that had never been done before. For me, one of the exciting things was being able to listen to the music for the films being played on a Moviola, which is a terrible way to listen to music! I kept thinking how wonderful it was and that no one outside of those walls had ever heard it before. I was very impressed with that.

JP: I ask everybody this because it's something I wish I could have done. Did you attend the premiere of *Snow White*?

Things were a lot different in those days. We couldn't afford tickets and they sure weren't free! It was very cold and we didn't have very warm clothes. We went down to the Carthay Circle Theatre and watched Walt and a few of the top people and some of the movie stars go in...then we left! [Laughter.]

JP: The people responsible for this beautiful film didn't get to see it?

I think that was along the same lines as not giving artists screen credit. I don't think Walt ever wanted that. His feeling was the name "Walt Disney" represented all of us. Walt was hanging by his teeth financially, and really, I think he was for most of his career. Not at all like today. The interest in these things is incredible. The *Bambi* videocassette sold 10 million copies, breaking all previous records!

JP: After *Snow White*, did you work with Grim on other projects?

After *Snow White*, Grim worked on a couple of shorts and I assisted him on them. *Ferdinand the Bull* was one. I worked on the scene where the women are coming in. We also worked on *Mother Goose Goes Hollywood*, using caricatures by T. Hee. Grim and I did "Three Men In a Tub", who were Charles Laughton, Freddie Bartholomew, and Spencer Tracy. We also did W. C. Fields and Charlie McCarthy.

JP: Was it after finishing these that you began work on *Bambi*?

Yes, Walt wanted to do another picture. *Pinocchio* and *Fantasia* were being made at the same time. There were groups working on *Fantasia*. Top animators, such as Milt Kahl, were working on *Pinocchio*, along with Frank Thomas, Woolie Reitherman, and Bill Tytla.

JP: Who were the animators you worked with on *Bambi*?

Milt Kahl, Frank Thomas, Ollie Johnston, and myself did most of the animation on *Bambi*; a rather small group that helped, I think, to maintain its consistency. There was no hurry in getting something for the top animators to do, as opposed to, say, *The Little Mermaid*. I'm not saying it isn't a fine feature, because it is, but I can see that each scene was done by someone else because of the drawing inconsistencies. It's just a little different than I would conceive a character, and it certainly meets with the public's appreciation.

Bambi required a whole new look with highly specialized people who could draw animals. These were not the guys who were working on the Donald and Mickey cartoons. I worked for three years in Story for *Bambi*, and it was one of the few times I was able to use my knowledge of animal anatomy. Walt saw the drawings I had done and said he wanted to see my work on the screen. He put me in with his top animators and told them to teach me how to animate. Once again, this was with a very small staff, and this, as with *Snow White*, presented a terrible drawing problem. I spent six years of my life on *Bambi*.

JP: *Bambi* was an unusual project from what the studio had previously been involved with: a pastoral wildlife story.

Yes, and to do it so it could be believed. The thing is, if these true-to-life characters don't look believable, then the whole thing falls apart; it doesn't matter how funny the stuff is. If you look at the model sheets on *Snow White* as compared to the ones for *Bambi*, the jump is enormous; getting the plasticity into the characters and making them personalities. None of the wildlife characters in *Snow White* were characters, they just filled an important part of the picture. There was a group of us who used to go to zoos together. On the weekends, we'd go down to the San Diego Zoo or to a place out in the valley called Goebel's Lion Farm. The Griffith Park Zoo was very minimal at the time, but still—it was animals. When we were working on *Bambi*, we had two fawns brought in from New England, even though the original story was in Germany. I don't know why it was changed. They used a white-tailed deer, which is very beautiful, and we had our "deodorized" skunk and rabbits, all of these animals to study. Eventually the deer was given to the Griffith Park Zoo.

JP: As well as working on the story, you designed most of the *Bambi* characters.

Throughout my career, when I was finished with the drawing for one film I would go up to the Story Department and help develop sequences. Sometimes, these were for scenes that I would animate later on. I did the designs for the young Bambi and both Flower the Skunk and Thumper the Rabbit, though they were further developed by other people. For example, the final Bambi model sheet was very much Milt Kahl's work, and I think for Thumper, also. The skunk was mine from beginning to end, and I animated a lot of him.

JP: Besides the manpower shortages, do you recall any other problems with making the film?

I don't recall that there were. As I say, George Stallings and I had worked in Story. We did the love sequence with Thumper and Flower. I think that was the sequence that convinced Walt to make an animator out of me. I also did the sequence of the skunk hibernating. I did some Thumper scenes and of Bambi and Faline as well. I developed what I thought was a sexy walk for Faline which was perhaps like a high-fashion model might have walked. It was very hard work, but it paid off.

JP: Do you have a favorite sequence in *Bambi*?

Not really. When you've done these things, there's really nothing like getting them on to the big screen and seeing an audience's reaction for the first time, especially with humor. [The] Grauman's Chinese [Theatre] premiere of *Bambi* would certainly be up there. We came to the part of the film I had worked on where the two skunks fall in love. You see the two tails walk off together through the flowers and then Flower stands up, and my God—the laugh it got! I'm crying and everyone in the place is laughing! One of the fellows summed it up perfectly when he said, "We'll never experience anything like this again as long as we live."

JP: Making it ironic is that this beautiful film was financially disappointing, as were *Pinocchio* and *Fantasia*.

Yes, because of the war. Disney had made such a great deal of money on *Snow White* that the banks gave him the go-ahead on the next three films. But he was heavily dependent on the foreign market. He even made a point to record soundtracks in several languages. We also had to be careful of physical gestures that could be interpreted as offensive in another country. In *Cinderella*, Kimball had one of the mice give the "OK" sign with his fingers. It turns out that in Brazil that means something… not very nice, so we had to change it. We always had to watch for those kinds of things. When the war came in 1941, Disney lost the entire foreign market, and the foreign market was so important to Disney. Would the studio be able to survive? I don't know how many years it took just to pay back the cost of having the Philadelphia Symphony record the *Fantasia* soundtrack, and for the prints and so forth! Now, of course, it's accepted as being one of Walt's greatest movies, which of course I think it is.

JP: There was talk of a sequel to *Fantasia*. What do you know of that?

I had heard that and ran into Walt while going into the studio one day. I told him I had an idea for another *Fantasia*. I wanted to do a thing out of *Scheherazade*, *Ali Baba and the 40 Thieves*, and those wonderful romantic stories. Walt said, "My God, Marc, I don't dare go to the stockholders with that. They're still skinning me alive for the first one!" So I never had a chance to [work on a sequel.].

JP: During World War II, the studio turned its attention from feature animation to primarily training and propaganda films made for the government. What was the studio like during that period?

The studio actually became something of a military reserve unit. Many of us went into the service. I was supposed to go into the Marine Corps. They had offered me a sergeancy, but I would be doing the same thing for them as I was doing for Disney. Anyway, it was decided that we should stay with the studio. The films we worked on were things we did for the Navy on the Battles of the Coral Sea and Midway. The fighter pilots who had fought and won these battles, in really inferior planes, came to the studio and worked with us. We put all of their experiences and theories into animation so that others could understand them. They were distributed to the Army Air Corps and others. We made *Rules of the Nautical Road* and films used to train sea captains who commanded the Liberty Ships. These were being made out of concrete and being sunk as fast as they could be built. We made films about mosquito abatement for areas prone to malaria, yellow fever, and so on. We did pictures about growing food in what would be referred to today as Third World countries. We really had an amazing group of people there; about half college professors and half military brass. They had Walt very disenchanted most of the time. [Laughter]

JP: There were actually armed soldiers on the lot?

Oh, yes, you needed a pass to go from one building to another! We had the Norden Bombsight, which was the best bombsight in the world at that time. I was brought in and was under armed guard from morning until evening. We all had to go through FBI and military checks.

JP: Your most well-known film from the war years is, of course, *Victory Through Air Power*.

When I saw *Victory Through Air Power* at Grauman's Egyptian Theatre, there were these people sitting in front of me who turned out to be Alfred Hitchcock and his wife and daughter. I admired his work so very much that seeing him so effusive about our film was very nice.

JP: Did you go on the South American tour with Walt in 1941? The *Good Will* shorts were a result of those.

No, I didn't go on that, but I knew everybody who did, and I would have loved to have gone. They made *Saludos Amigos*, and with the little bit that was left over came *The Three Caballeros*. They came back with a lot of top Latin musicians and they worked with us and were here for quite a while. They worked on a good many other things besides.

JP: There were no features made during the War, but the studio did manage to produce a few things for commercial release.

During the War, they made several pictures that were made up of short subjects—*Make Mine Music* and so on. They tied together a bunch of them and made a full program. But to tell a story from beginning to end, it was *Song of the South*, which is basically a live-action film with little Uncle Remus stories told through animation.

JP: With *Song of the South*, Walt started venturing into live-action films. Do you think perhaps he was hesitant about another animated feature after three financial failures?

I think live action was something Walt always wanted to do and it took a long time for people to come around to letting him do that. We kind of had to take the back door in for a while. With *Song of the South*, we began branching out slowly into live action. We were a little disappointed in the live-action sequences, which were just not up to par for a number of reasons. The cinematographer on that was Gregg Toland, who had worked with Orson Welles on *Citizen Kane*, and whose work on the picture I thought was just great. We also did *So Dear To My Heart* with Bobby Driscoll and Burl Ives, but as usual people would say, "But Mr. Disney, you're known for your animation." We never really had the opportunity until we found we had something in Great Britain called "blocked money"; that is, money that cannot leave the British Isles. So they sent Bobby Driscoll and the writer, producer, and director and made some pretty good films over there, mostly British themes such as *Treasure Island* with an all-British cast. This was the beginning of Walt Disney getting into live-action films. I went over and visited a few times. It was interesting to see how other people worked. I still think it's a great picture.

JP: What sequences did you animate on *Song of the South*?

I worked on some of the little stories, and I animated what I think is the first sequence in the picture where the bear and fox are down in the cave making the Tar Baby. The buttons are pulled off the bear's coat for eyes, then you hear a cry offstage, and the bear has no hair on his fanny, and that becomes the Tar Baby's hair. That got a hell of a big laugh. These were great characters to work with, and it was interesting since it was the first feature film we'd done in awhile.

JP: I know a former Disney staffer who recalls helping to develop the Uncle Remus characters as early as 1939. I also believe work on *Peter Pan* and *Alice in Wonderland* commenced around then also, yet these films were not made until many years later.

Many of these things were worked on over long periods of time and then set aside. This happened all the time. Walt would say, "Why don't we work on this for awhile?", or he'd see it just wasn't right for the moment. He had an apartment at the studio where he could stay overnight. He used to go around the rooms and look over the story work. If it was coming along, he'd leave you alone. Sometimes you wouldn't see him for months, then his secretary would call and tell you that you had a meeting with him that afternoon to show him what you were working on. If he liked what you did and really got hot on it, he'd be in your office morning, noon, and night. He wanted to stay right on top of the story because that was his great strength, his story work. He was a great storyteller and could act out what the characters were doing very well. Sometimes you wondered if you could animate them as well as he could act them out. [Laughter] This was a genuine talent that he had. He had little interest in stylized things, and he enjoyed things that you did and brought to life. He considered himself basically a storyman, not an animator.

JP: Besides the *Fantasia* sequence, can you recall other shelved projects of yours that you would have liked to have seen go into production?

Oh, yes—a number of them. We did a thing right after the War about man going into space. *Life* magazine had done a series of articles on the subject, which I thought was just marvelous. I thought it would have adapted to animation very easily, where we could show things being shot into space and getting to the point where there is no gravity. I clipped a lot of articles about it from the newspaper, and I remember one in particular where someone wanted to patent the idea of letting sheep and cows graze on the moon! I collected all this material together and one morning I ran into Walt while walking into the studio, and I said, "Hey, Walt—I've got a great idea for a film!", and I explained it to him. He was so fed up with the people who had been quartered there during the War—the generals and colonels and professors who had taken over his office—that he said, "I never want to make another educational film as long as I live!" [Laughter.]

I slowly learned that it was a mistake to talk to Walt about making a film. You had to show him. Not much later, George Pal made a film about a trip to the moon, and later Kimball made a kind of crazy one about a moon flight. By that time, the excitement was gone. If we had done it earlier, we would have been the first.

JP: Can we talk a bit about the first big success of the post-war years, *Cinderella*? You were very heavily involved in the production of that film.

I worked on that from beginning to end. I did story work on it and I set the style for Cinderella herself. I worked on the scene where the mice make her dress and I animated the sequence where she runs down to show it to her stepsisters and they tear it off her. I did the stepsisters as well as the segment where Cinderella runs out into the garden and drops onto the stone bench. I came up with the idea that when the Fairy Godmother appeared, Cinderella's head would be in her lap. I thought that would be a good way to bring her into the scene. I did that sequence all the way through except for Milt Kahl, who did the Fairy Godmother. John Lounsbery did the transformation of the animals, and I did up to where she got her gown from the Fairy Godmother. Someone told me once they had eaten lunch with Walt and a lady asked him what his favorite piece of animation was. Walt replied, "When Cinderella got her gown." I think this is a nice story, not only because I animated that scene, but it really shows a lot about Walt Disney himself: magic, wishes coming true, and that kind of thing. Cinderella had a real strength of character throughout that film. They weren't going to beat her, no matter what. She was a tough little dame! [Laughter]

JP: You also worked on one of my favorites, *Alice in Wonderland*. What did you do on *Alice*?

I did a kind of crazy sequence with the Mad Hatter and the March Hare. I also did the scene in the woods, and all these strange creatures that look like spectacles are landing on her head.

JP: When you're adapting a story for animation that is very well known, such as *Alice* or *Peter Pan*, how much liberty do you feel you may take with the story and characters?

Well, with something like *Alice in Wonderland*, there is an entire cult out there who thinks it's the greatest thing in the world and that John Tenniel's drawings are the only ones for Alice, and I kind of go along with them. The Duchess and the other characters were marvelous, and I don't think we even came close to that in the film. I think it's a good film, and I enjoy it now more than I did then. None of us liked it when it first came out, and we thought it was a pretty poorly done film—and from a purist point of view, it is. It was a situation where you take this little girl and throw her into a madhouse. There's no opportunity for her to be warm; perhaps if she had her cat with her. The entire cast is made up of these entirely unsympathetic characters who don't understand her, and she certainly doesn't understand them. It was very difficult to do. I have a tape of the picture and when I look at it, it doesn't bother me as much now as it did then. But at the time an awful lot of us had the feeling that we were disappointed in it. We always expected more of ourselves. We always expected everything to come off better than it did. I think part of that attitude came from Walt himself, which was, "Oh, well, the next one will be better."

JP: For *Peter Pan* you designed Tinker Bell, who almost rivals Mickey himself as the symbol of Disney animation. She has been called a tiny Marilyn Monroe. Did you set out to make her a sexy character?

In the script they asked for certain business to be done, and one of them was that she lands on a mirror and sees that her hips are a little broad. So you don't have a choice—you've got to show her hips, it's written in the script. [Laughter] They also made a point of showing that Tinker Bell is very jealous of Wendy. Actually, I enjoyed doing her.

Some people may ask, "Just what does a directing animator do?" He sets the characters of the film, but will also animate critical personality scenes. I did the scenes of Tinker Bell where she had close contact with Peter Pan or the kids. I did the drawer scene and the sequence in Captain Hook's cabin where she's sitting on a bottle telling him where Peter's hideout is. When I got to that scene sitting on the bottle, I was able to slim her down a bit. Sometimes you get locked into things like this early in the picture, and it gets inked and painted. I'm not unhappy with it, but those are just the types of things that happen when you're in production.

JP: Before talking about *Sleeping Beauty*, could you give us a brief description of your usual production methods on the features?

It would really depend on what you happened to be working on. Generally, you would have one top assistant and he would have two or three assistants under him who most of the time were in-betweeners. Never a large operation, really. Since I was involved with the animation of so many humans there was generally some live-action footage to work from or some sort of footage you looked over. Someone asked me just the other day, "Didn't you fellows just rotoscope everything?", and that's a term I dislike immensely. When you just trace over film footage, everything has a tendency to become very broad. Every woman you drew would turn out looking like this Roseanne character on television. I see quite a lot of this thing on Saturday morning cartoons where they've worked from live footage and it has a very traced look about it and it looks dead. Live action shows people doing things and it's right on the nose. However, in animation, I try to stay two or three frames ahead of everything; action, then reaction. You're talking about 24 frames per second that are going through the projector, so it's a minute thing that you really can't see. It's highly synchronized. Action that is difficult to do, such as a dancer, I would want to see a performer do it and then look at the film, not trace it. This is very true with my Cruella de Vil for *101 Dalmatians*. We had a wonderful actress, Mary Wickes, who did some great live action. I used her suggestions and made them more so. If you looked at the footage of Mary and then the character, you would have a difficult time seeing the resemblance. It's suggestion you need, and that's why I dislike the term "rotoscope". Live action may be used as a blueprint, as a reference, but never traced. I see some of our films now and it's easy to spot who was doing that sort of thing.

JP: Earlier you commented that Walt had no interest in highly stylized things, but yet I would call *Sleeping Beauty* highly stylized with a very non-Disney look to it.

It's stylized but in a different way. The characters come to life even though they are drawn a little differently and are three-dimensional. They don't live in a flat world. The style we came up with for that was predicated a lot by the fact that the man doing the background, Eyvind Earle, had a strong style that Walt liked. Of course, *Sleeping Beauty* was the first wide-screen feature we ever did.[1] Walt told us, "You don't have to cut all of the time. Think of the film as a moving illustration." We were very concerned about how to "cut" on the wide screen. We soon discovered that it was just the same as you would on anything else. So we didn't cut…and we didn't cut…and finally Walt said, "For God's sake, Marc, why didn't you cut?!" [Laughter] After that, we didn't worry about the wide screen any more. It looked to me like looking through a mail box. The main thing was keeping your action within the confines of regular proportion. A lot of that film has been consequently cut down for videocassettes. I think the artists make a terrible mistake when they put a lot of action on the ends of the screen. When it gets cut down, there won't be anything left but the background.

JP: For *Sleeping Beauty* you designed the most chilling villainess of them all, Maleficent the Sorceress. How did you create her unique appearance?

I sat down and went through a lot of material I had, including a book of Czechoslovakian religious paintings. There was this figure with the red and black drapery in the back that looked like flames that I thought would be great to use. I took the idea of the collar partly from a bat, and the horns looked like a devil. I received a card recently from Eleanor Audley, who did the voice of Maleficent. She's 84 years old and I guess quite ill. She was a very fine actress and not at all dependent on what we were doing. [Laughter.]

---

1 In reality, *Lady and the Tramp* had earlier been released in CinemaScope.

JP: The last animated feature you worked on was *101 Dalmatians* in 1961.

Yes, that was my last, and I think I enjoyed working on Cruella more than any of the others. The broadest thing I ever had a chance to do was Cruella, and I enjoyed that aspect of her. She also operated without magic, unlike characters in *Sleeping Beauty*, *Alice*, or *Cinderella*. She was just a nutty woman who probably went to the bathroom just like the rest of us. No magic there! [Laughter] She had no realization whatsoever that she was cruel. That's just the way she was. She had no idea that the killing and butchering of these little puppies for a coat involved pain and suffering. She's pure evil, and that's what makes her interesting.

JP: *Dalmatians* was also the debut film for Ub Iwerks' cel-photocopying technique.[2]

Yes, and if I had it to do over again, I think I would work a little cleaner than I did. I did all of Cruella de Vil, every scene of her. I had assistants at the time who were more inclined to just touch up my drawings, which were frequently a little rough. There is some roughness on the screen in some of my stuff that I don't like and that I regret. There was something used on this film that the artists liked but Walt didn't, which was using lines for backgrounds. I thought it was very good because for the first time the drawings in the front matched the drawings in the back. There had always been these super-delicate tones in the backgrounds, and then a hard cartoon line around the characters. To me, they never seemed consistent. With *Bambi*, I think we did quite well because we used a colored line.

JP: Let's talk about some of your studio colleagues. Why don't we start with Walt Kelly? Did you know him?

I knew Walt Kelly very well. We both came to the studio at around the same time and were great friends in the early days. We both had the same story aspirations, and we did some stories together and presented them, not too successfully. [Laughter] We did some things that were akin to his later work on Pogo, sort of a hound-dog thing in the South. I don't remember too much about the story, except there was a fire engine in it and something else. I can't remember exactly. I still slap myself. Walt [Kelly] came back from the East and was working on something for Chuck Jones. He sent the word around that he sure would like to see Marc Davis. I would have loved to have seen him, but I didn't do it, and not too long after that he died. I'm still sore at myself for that.

---

2 The Xerox process had been tested earlier in some scenes of *Sleeping Beauty*.

The studio was a funny place to work because you would be close to someone you were working with. Then if you were put into something else, you wouldn't see them anymore because now you were working with these other people. They wouldn't see you because they were now seeing the people around them.

JP: One of my old idols, Virgil Partch, also got his start at Disney.

Virgil came from Los Angeles and studied at Chouinard's. He had become sort of famous for swallowing the goldfish in the pond there. [Laughter] He was a wonderful guy and an assistant to Ollie Johnston. He used to do these crazy little drawings. I still have a number of them around somewhere.

JP: Did you team up on any projects like you did with Kelly?

No, we were just good friends. I was looking at one of his old drawings just the other day. When he went into the Army, we gave him a big going-away party. Frank and Ollie were there, and it was at the Cock and Bull Restaurant down on the end of the Sunset Strip. When he came back after the war, he really took off on the cartooning thing. I did do the animation for a story of his called *Duck Pimples*. It wasn't a great effort [laughter] and it was certainly very different!

JP: While making *Bambi*, you worked with one of the very few female animators, Retta Scott.

Yes, they were rare. Retta had been a student at Chouinard's, and she used to go with us on our drawing trips. She could draw as well as any man. One of the things she did on *Bambi* was a bunch of hound dogs which was very powerful and frightening. I believe she's still in the business and lives up in the Bay area.

JP: Did you know another female Disney artist, Mary Blair?

I knew Mary very well. She was an extraordinary artist, and Walt thought very highly of her. She was the most amazing colorist of all time. I don't think even Matisse could hold a candle to her—and I mean that very sincerely. She could put colors together and they would just sing. Her work was generally quite stylized. A lot of people with limited backgrounds never really knew how to interpret things she did and how to get the most out of them. Her images tended to be flat. She did a lot of sketches where her images are still superb. I think things had to be planned a little differently in order to take advantage of that. She did an awful lot of the South American things and went on that trip [to South America] with some of the other artists and story men.

JP: A much lesser-known artist, Jesse Marsh, also worked at Disney for a while.

He worked in the Animation Department with Ward Kimball for a long time. Ward knew him very well. After he left the studio, he worked on the *Tarzan* comic books for many years. He was a very talented draftsman and used to decorate the doors of our studios with huge color nudes drawn on wrapping paper. He was very good! [Laughter]

JP: Marsh died fairly young before he could be recognized at all. He has a small but devout following of his minimalist style.

The longevity of these people, so many of them came to tragic endings—Freddie Moore, Woolie Reitherman, Virg Partch—all tragedies. Walt Kelly wasn't that old.

JP: Do you have a favorite piece of animation by one of your colleagues?

I have a print of *Saludos Amigos*. There's a sequence Milt Kahl worked on with Donald Duck crossing a chasm on the back of a llama. It's the funniest piece of animation I think I've ever seen. Just wonderful. Milt was a fantastic animator and perhaps my closest friend at the studio.

JP: Was there competition among the Disney artists?

There was competition, but it was an odd kind of competition. I've said before in a joking manner that Walt Disney's greatest achievement was in getting us all to work together without killing one another! The biggest problem with animation is getting a group of people who can work together. There is something about being an artist...you have to believe in yourself and believe in what you are doing. If it isn't there, you won't try to do anything. Taking people from all over the world and getting them to come here and work together and make a picture at the end was a very remarkable thing! Walt had a smart idea that everybody should call each other by their first names, including him. He felt the terms "Mister" and "Miss" put up an immediate barrier and that it's pretty hard to get angry with someone when you're calling them by their first names. Making an animated film is almost like crocheting; it's all done by hand. Also various talents will take you in different directions. It isn't like an actor who can say, "I can do this part 10 different ways." You have to figure out one way to do it and stick with it.

JP: Years ago you said, "Animation is anachronism. A hand-made commodity in a mechanized world." With the creation of computerized animation is the craft merely catching up with the times?

If we were doing something today such as *Victory Through Air Power*, we would no doubt have a lot of the chart work done by computers, which I don't particularly like, since a computer can't know what I think. I don't think you're going to be able to sit down at a computer and turn out a *Mona Lisa* or a piece of Milt Kahl animation. You have to have a heart in there somewhere.

JP: Hasn't the success of *The Simpsons* and similar programs proven that drawing isn't important anymore?

I feel pretty much the same way about that as I do about this *Garfield* thing that Jim Davis does. It's just not my cup of tea. Also, *Who Framed Roger Rabbit?* does not reflect my point of view on animation. I go along with what Walt Disney wanted to do, which was bring things to life, anything, to make it live. I feel that as an artist I have a knowledge of how things move and work. I have the ability to draw anything. I can go away from that and become as zany as you like, but I always have that center to come back to. I feel strongly about that, but I'm of a different generation. The films we worked on, now referred to as classic Disney animation, hold up very well. Walt had a clever idea, and that was to never allow any current slang in the films. I heard an expression on the radio the other day: "Get a life." This is exactly the type of thing we would have never used in our pictures. This is the kind of thing that will date the film.

JP: After you completed your work on *101 Dalmatians*, your career at Disney took a different turn. How did that come about?

There was a thought among the business people at the studio that perhaps Walt should discontinue doing feature animation. As I mentioned before, I would usually finish work on one film and then start work on another. But after *Dalmatians*, Walt told me to go down to Disneyland and look over the Nature's Wonderland attraction. I did, and came back with a bunch of drawings on it. It turned out he just wanted me to look it over and tell him how great it was. Anyway, I looked at it quite critically and came up with a lot of opinions. I started going down the list of what was wrong with the attraction. The first thing on the list was the mining car. The seats have you sitting face-to-face with total strangers, and you have to crane your neck to see the attraction, and you can't physically turn around to see what's behind you. I told Walt seeing ahead of you is a natural instinct of self-preservation, which it is. He bought that. There were two kit foxes about a hundred feet apart. One would move his head from side to side and the other moved his head up and down. I put them together and this immediately creates a little tableau with one saying "yes" and the other saying "no". I went through the whole attraction and did little things like that, and Walt thought it was great. After that, he became very interested in staging things from the point of view from which you were looking at it. That was the beginning. We worked on all four attractions at the New York World's Fair at the same time.

JP: One of your most popular efforts was *Great Moments With Mr. Lincoln*. How did that come about?

Because of my knowledge as an animator, I was teaching a very advanced course on movement one night a week at Chouinard's when Walt announced he wanted to construct a Lincoln figure. He asked me to give it some thought, and I did a folder full of drawings on how to articulate a mechanical man. It turns out I was totally wrong. We weren't building a mechanical man. We weren't doing a *Metropolis*; we were creating an illusion of Abraham Lincoln. We managed to get this thing worked out and ready for the World's Fair. At the premiere the figure stood up, took a step forward, and delivered his speech in a very lifelike manner. A reviewer for *The New York Times* wrote that the figure was so good that he believed it walked forward on the stage, and it came off very well.

JP: I was at Disneyland recently. On the Mr. Lincoln attraction they went to great lengths to explain how the new figure is an improvement over the original. I didn't like it as well as the original, and I believe they changed the dialogue, which had been very inspiring.

I don't go down there any more. It upsets me. The beauty of our Mr. Lincoln was in its subtlety of movement. I laid this thing out like a scene of animation on paper; every word he said and how he should move. The fellows who programmed it followed my layouts just like an animator would follow an exposure sheet or a musician would follow a sheet of music.

JP: You developed another popular attraction as well, Pirates of the Caribbean.

Walt asked me to begin work on a walk-through attraction based on the Pirates of the Caribbean. While I was working on it, he would come into my office and had to force himself not to look at the boards; he wasn't ready to see them yet. Unfortunately, Walt never lived to see that attraction completed. I did a walk-through with him before any of the figures or backgrounds were in place. The auction scene was partially assembled over at WED and he saw that. Then, unfortunately, he died, and that was the end of his participation.

JP: Do you recall how you heard of Walt's passing?

I was in my office at the studio. One of the men whose sister was nurse at St. Joseph's Hospital across the street from the studio called to say that Walt Disney had just died. It was a shocker. What now? That was in 1966 and I left in 1978, but before I left, I worked on the It's A Small World attraction, as well as America Sings, and the Country Bear Jamboree, which was designed strictly for the Florida park.

JP: Considering all the films that have been made since 1940, I think it's ironic that as we sit here today 50 years later, those rumors about a *Fantasia* sequel are still with us.

I heard the rumors, and I think current management would do anything if they thought they could make it go. At least they're keeping animation on the market, which is good. It disappoints me a lot in a lot of ways because I think they're trying to rush them into doing a feature a year. You can do a feature a year if you have the amount of people and talent to do that. But right now, a lot of those people are either being trained or are training themselves in animation. I don't think there are people there who can help them. Eric Larson, who passed away not too long ago, stayed on for quite a long time helping the young people. When they moved animation from the studio and over to Glendale into the Walt Disney Imagineering area, it hurt him a great deal and he decided to retire. Not long after that he became ill and died, unfortunately.

JP: Precisely how would you characterize your association with the studio these days?

I think they consider me a consultant, though I am doing a lot less of that sort of thing now. Joe Grant gives them story help when they ask for it. I went out a couple of months ago, and Joe and I critiqued a film they were working on. We gave them our ideas and we enjoyed ourselves. They need guidance that they just haven't had. There is no one that can give it to them, except a few, and they're not going to sit there and do that. There are a lot of things here I want to work on on my own, including some painting. That's why I have so many things lying around, as you can see. I want to look them over and see how I want to approach them. I think I'm finally getting to the point where I'm starting to get them right!

JP: Not long ago you were honored at a special ceremony at the studio that paid tribute to the Nine Old Men as well as Ub Iwerks. How does it feel to be a historic figure?

It makes you feel old! [Laughter] It's nice that people recognize our work. It was a very strange business in that we were kept anonymous throughout our entire careers. This wasn't too happy for artists who would have liked to have signed their work and see their names on the screen just like anyone else. To find that we're getting credit for what we did is a far cry from the old days, when everybody thought Walt Disney did all the drawing!

© 2004 John Province

Marc Davis (1913–2000)

Interviewed by Michael Lyons on March 27, 1998

When Marc Davis taught at the Chouinard Art Institute in Los Angeles, one of his students was Bob Kurtz. This student would go on to become an award-winning animator with his own studio and years later would remember Davis fondly.

"Animators get cast like actors," said Kurtz, adding, "there are certain roles you wouldn't put them in. But it's difficult to think of a role Marc couldn't handle. To use a baseball analogy, he's not just the team's utility player, he's the pitcher, the batter, and the fielder all in one."[1]

A perfect analogy indeed for one of the greatest talents to work in animation. It's no wonder that Walt Disney once called Marc his "Renaissance Man".

Unfortunately we lost Marc Davis on January 12, 2000, after a long battle with cancer. With Marc's passing, the world lost a real master of the medium and a true gentleman as well.

Michael Lyons had the good fortune to sit down and talk with Marc while he was at Walt Disney World in Florida in March 1998 for an event celebrating Marc's 85th birthday.

Michael Lyons: First off, you started at the Disney studio in 1935, correct?

Marc Davis: Yes, December 2nd of 1935.

ML: What was the studio like then?

Well, it was a very interesting place. During the early days of Disney, the women were all in Ink and Paint. The men were either in some part of Story or Animation. This was kind of like a nunnery and a monastery.

Before I came to the studio, Walt Disney did a film called *The Three Little Pigs*. This went around the world and was an incredible success, especially the song, "Who's Afraid of the Big Bad Wolf". And everybody at the time had the wolf at their door, and that film meant a lot to me.

Then, there was another film. This man I knew who owned a theater called me up one day and said, "There's this film here that I want you

---

1 Bob Kurtz to Michael Lyons, March, 1998.

to see. I think you should be working for Walt Disney." The film was *Who Killed Cock Robin?* I went over to see it, and I thought it was damn good. So I decided to give it a try and go out to Los Angeles. My father had died and I was taking care of my mother, so we decided to drive down to Los Angeles. That's how I got this job, and I'm very glad I did.

Walt Disney knew that he wanted to do a feature film, and when I went there he had already started *Snow White and the Seven Dwarfs*. He was looking for artists, so he advertised all over the world in the classified section, "Walt Disney Wants Artists". At the time, most of the people in the animation business were newspaper artists. These guys weren't really trained artists, and Walt was looking for somebody to bring these characters to life. That's where I came in. At that time, it was the Depression; a horrible time. Most of the guys at the studio made fifteen dollars a week. I got twenty-two because I was a "better-trained" artist. I knew human anatomy and animal anatomy. That's how I ended up on *Bambi* because I had that background.

He had a man there at the time who was a drawing instructor. His name was Don Graham. Your first two weeks at the Studio was like being back at art school. Don was a marvelous man, and he was the one who judged. I went through this training, so I ended up working on "the Girl" in *Snow White*.

ML: That was with Grim Natwick, is that correct?

Yeah, he was my first boss there. Grim was an older man, a marvelous man. I ended up working with him. After *Snow White* was made, Grim decided that he had had enough and he left, but he and I remained very good friends. A few years back, we had a one hundred-year birthday party for Grim, and that was great. I gave a talk and I said, "Ya know, people have asked me, 'What did I learn from Grim Natwick?" I said, "Well, the first thing is, I learned to drink wine. I knew wine was red and it came in a two-quart bottle. Grim taught me that wine was many colors and came in smaller bottles." He absolutely loved that.

ML: Five years after *Snow White* came *Bambi*. That was the film in which Walt Disney moved you on to animator, correct?

After *Snow White* came out and was a success, they began work on *Pinocchio* and they were also working on *Fantasia*. They also put some people to work on story for *Bambi*, and I was one of those people. They moved us up to the middle of Hollywood, [to] an old studio that some-body else had at the time.[2] When the lease ran out, we were the first

---

2 See note 18 from interview with Rudolf Ising.

people to move into the new studio. This was the first time Walt saw what I could do as an artist. I did the young animals in the story, and apparently, he was delighted with my drawings and said, "I want to see this guy's drawings on the screen. Make an animator out of him." So I was trained by a few of the other animators like Milt Kahl and Frank Thomas, and I stayed on *Bambi* for six years.

We moved out to the new studio and we were up on the third floor, 3D wing, and Walt had his apartment and he would stay overnight. The man who was story director on *Bambi* was Perce Pearce; he had also been story director on *Snow White*. He would stand in the hallway when he knew Walt was coming, and he'd say, "Man is in the forest! Man is in the forest!" He was quite a marvelous man. So somewhere along there, Walt became so fascinated with my drawings. He said, "Let's make an animator out of him." So, I'm glad that he did this for me.

ML: After working in animation, you went to work on the theme park attractions?

First thing I did was the four attractions for the New York World's Fair. After that, he had me working on attractions for Disneyland.

Every time I finished animating a film, I'd go up to the story department and start work on another one. This was very different from the other animators. In fact, Walt once called Alice[3] over to look at some of my drawings,and he said, "Marc's my Renaissance Man. He can do anything. All of these other animators can do one thing, they can animate. Marc can do anything." That was very typical of Walt. You'd have a meeting with him and then an hour or so later someone would knock on your door and say, "Boy, Marc, did you ever have a great meeting with Walt!" He found it difficult to compliment anyone directly to their face.

ML: Tell me a little bit about Imagineering, or WED, when you first started there.

The average story that we would use is far removed from what they use today. They had things like The House of Tomorrow. One of the first things that I worked on was the Jungle Cruise.

It bothered me that on a lot of the attractions, the animals were going to be created by using real animal skins. I didn't think it was right that Disneyland should kill animals for entertainment. So I found out that you could do a pretty good job with artificial fur and it worked out a lot better.

---

3 Marc's wife, Alice Davis. Alice Davis is a Disney Legend in her own right, having designed the costumes for It's a Small World and Pirates of the Caribbean.

ML: I have to ask—I heard a story about *Pirates of the Caribbean*, that one of the pirates was based on a janitor who used to work at Disney.

Yeah. [Laughs] That was John the janitor. He's one of the three guys in the jail who is trying to get the dog to come over with the key. The guy in the middle is John.

ML: I had read a quote from you about *Sleeping Beauty*'s Maleficent, where you said, "All she did was stand around making speeches and delivering curses. She had very little intimate contact with the other characters." Was the character a challenge for you?

Well, the hardest thing with Maleficent was how to bring her to life. She *did* stand up and make speeches, but that's when I introduced the Raven. This way she could work with the Raven. She also had a wonderful voice, Eleanor Audley, wonderful lady.

ML: What do you think it takes, in your opinion to be a good animator?

Well, you have to create characters as an artist, but you also have to be able to bring them to life. If you pleased Walt Disney, you were bringing things to life.

There was this toward the end of his life when I was working at WED. Walt came into my office with some people and said to them, "You guys go on, I'd like to talk to Marc." So I showed him the drawings I had done, which later became the Country Bear Jamboree. He laughed and chuckled. Walt was like a child at Christmas. As long as he had another present to unwrap, he was happy. So afterwards, I asked him if he'd like to go out into the shop. We went in there and we looked at what we had done for Flight to the Moon. We were only there a few minutes, and Walt looked very tired and he said, "Could someone take me back to the studio?" And there was no lack of offers to do that. I headed back to my office, and then Walt stopped. He turned and said, "Goodbye Marc." And he died about three weeks later.

ML: And you had a sense...?

Oh, yeah. He never said "Goodbye." He'd say "Take it easy," "See you later," like that. He was a very special man. A guy like Walt only comes along every hundred years.

© 2004 Michael Lyons

Milt Kahl (1909–1987)

Interviewed by Robin Allan and Dr. William Moritz on June 9, 1985

Nicknamed the King of Kings, Milt Kahl, one of the famous Nine Old Men, was considered by many as the best draftsman of the Disney studio. Born on March 22, 1909, Milton Erwin Kahl started at Disney on June 25, 1934.

He worked as an inbetweener on *Mickey's Fire Brigade* (1935) and started animating on *Mickey's Circus* (1936), with various shorts following. When *Snow White* entered production, he joined the animator's team on Walt's first full-length feature.

His big break, however, came on the next movie, *Pinocchio*, where he was instrumental in redesigning the central character. From that point on, Milt Kahl worked on most of Disney's animated features and on quite a few shorts, including *Education for Death*, *The Winged Scourge*, and *Tiger Trouble*.

After WWII, he was often responsible for the final design of the characters for the animated features. His work on Shere Khan in *The Jungle Book* is often considered as the absolute masterpiece in Disney animation history.

Milt retired on April 30, 1976, after having animated the villain from *The Rescuers*, Medusa.

Robin Allan and the late Dr. William Moritz (1943–2004) conducted this interview at Milt's home in Marin County, California, as part of Robin's research for what would become the book *Walt Disney and Europe* (Indiana University Press, 1999).

Robin remembers "Milt Kahl as a rather abrasive character, full of sharp humour and undoubtedly somewhat arrogant, though I suppose he had reason to be pleased with himself as he was certainly one of Disney's most talented animators. He gave a lively interview, and was patient in answering all my questions. His house, unlike those of other Disney artists, was quite devoid of Disney art. He had his own wire sculptures of ballet dancers on display, but nothing else of his own artwork, and said that he had put all that stuff behind him. His interests now were boats and vintage cars. He showed me some caricatures of his colleagues, especially of his close friend Marc Davis and Ward Kimball."

Robin Allan: It would be nice to know what you liked in the way of art as a boy. You liked comic strips I believe.

Milt Kahl: I still enjoy some of the better comic strips. It amazes me that they can do these things day after day and be entertaining and funny. I liked the *Katzenjammer Kids*, I liked practically all of them. *Krazy Kat* was a wonderful one that George Herriman did. That's one of my all-time favourites, you know.

I was born in San Francisco. My parents were very poor. My father was an immigrant from Germany, born in Hamburg, and on my birth certificate he's a bartender. He drove limousines and became a superintendent at the place. I think his maximum salary was thirty-five dollars a week.

RA: He came from Germany as a young man?

That's right. At about twenty. My mother's parents were English. They were from Birmingham and came over here when they were quite young, too. She's completely English and he's German, with a Danish name, though.

RA: Did you draw and paint?

Oh, yes. I tore the paper up a lot. I used to draw motorcycles as a little kid. As soon as I became a professional, which was very young, too, I found it to be work. Most of these talented guys paint during weekends and love to draw. I have never liked to. Where I got my kicks in that field was to get a good performance on the screen and all my drawing was to that end.

RA: What about art books? Were your parents interested in them?

Not really. I think my father had a little talent. He used to do some newspaper ads for the company he worked for.

RA: Who were the most inspirational story people when you first joined Disney?

We didn't have any. When I first moved there, Walt was the one. There were also gag men: Ted Sears, Webb Smith.

RA: Where do you think this European feel and mood in *Snow White* and *Pinocchio* comes from. Is that Albert Hurter, do you think?

I think it no doubt had influence because a lot of the men which we had there, like Albert Hurter and Gustaf Tenggren, had European backgrounds. I think that's what influenced our studio European-wise, more than anything. But I don't think that consciously we have been influenced by European art.

RA: What did you do after *Pinocchio*?

I was involved with every feature except *Fantasia*, *Dumbo*, and *Victory Through Air Power*, heaven forbid.

As for *Bambi*, we had two units at the time. Maybe I did a short or two in between—doing in-between pictures happened to me once in a while. Then while *Fantasia* was being made, I was maybe actually finishing up on *Bambi* and then starting on, I believe it was *Wind in the Willows*.

RA: Yes. That was stop-started wasn't it?

We kinda overran on these things.

RA: Talking of Hurter and Tenggren, did you know them well?

Yes. I used to play chess with Gustaf.

I liked him very much. I remember he had a boat that he took us off to the Catalinas in. This thing had a skipper. It was a boat that had been used as a rum runner or something during prohibition and then they put a superstructure on it, cabins and stuff. So it made it top-heavy. And they put a lot of scrap iron in the bilges to balance it. Somebody had swiped a lot of that stuff out of there, and when we took that thing over to Catalina, it was not really seaworthy. It just rolled. It was terrible. That's the closest I've ever come in my whole life to becoming seasick.

RA: And Hurter?

You know, he was quite a good talent and a lot of the ideas in these pictures came from him. In *Snow White*, all these clocks. He could have been a cuckoo clockmaker.

He was a very argumentative fellow. He was always very eager to contest a point anytime. For instance, I remember when he asked Campbell Grant what time it was, and Campbell said, "Twelve minutes after ten," and he said, "Huh? Dat's right!" I think he took this old Big Ben out of his pocket.

Dr Moritz: Did he actually work on *Pinocchio* and *Snow White*?

Not on the animation. But a great many suggestions for things that could be in the background, what kind of clocks you'd have or what kind of chairs, what the carvings looked like on the chairs...in *Snow White* practically all that stuff is Albert Hurter's. All of it, in fact.

But in those days Walt really ruled the roost—a benign dictator. Somebody in the letters columns in the *Los Angeles Times* wrote in to suggest Walt as president. It's often been said that he wouldn't have made a good president, but he'd have made a hell of a good dictator. A benign dictator.

RA: Were you close to him in the early days?

I had no occasion to be. I was an in-betweener at the time.

RA: What about the Latin American pictures?

I didn't go down there with the team. I worked on "Lake Titicaca" for *Saludos Amigos*. I did the llama thing and some of the duck stuff and whatever happened to be pertinent to the llama. That was kinda fun.

RA: And *Three Caballeros*?

I don't think so. Wait a minute. I believe I did something on that... gee...I...I didn't like it very much, whatever it was. I can't even remember it. It was [an] in between pictures kind of a thing, you know.

RA: Tell us about Mary Blair.

She's a hell of an artist. Awfully talented. I knew her quite well. Marc Davis is a great admirer of Mary's, and justifiably so.

Marc himself is one hell of an artist, really. Goddamn good. We worked in adjoining rooms for a long time and knew each other very, very well. In fact, we had a kind of mutual admiration society. We always have had. I have a drawing here somewhere where he's standing behind my desk and I'm trying to figure out a cycle for "Pecos Bill", trying to work out this guy's hat flopping and something else going at the same time, and trying to arrange the drawings so that I can keep working them over and over again and having a hell of a time with it. And he's standing there saying, "If you were really God, these things would work out right in the first place."

RA: You mention *Pecos Bill*. Did you work on the musical compilation films? People tend to be hazy about them.

It's been so long ago. They showed the work-in-progress of *Snow White* to the staff for ARI [Audience Research]: part live action, part sketches, a Leica reel, a little hodgepodge of everything. Then they sent around questionnaires, and somebody said, "Stick to shorts." This rankled Walt. It just annoyed him to beat hell. And he never did find out who said that. But I remember, I think it was on *Melody Time*, they had this thing called "Bumble Boogie" with Freddy Martin. I thought it was just terrible, you know. Following this, we were having a story meeting on "Johnny Appleseed". We went in and Walt was already there. And, jeez, it just rankled me. So he says, "What's the matter with you?" And I said, "How could any sane man put his money in a piece of shit like that? I just can't understand it." So Walt said, "You're the son-of-a-bitch who said 'stick to shorts!'"

All those years he had accused quite a few people of it, but he never did find out who did it. It wasn't me.

So funny though. He was funny...Walt was an awfully funny guy. Especially when he was mad. Unless it was you his wrath was directed at. It's been directed at me an awful lot, but it didn't bother me very much. And another thing about Walt: he never held a grudge. He'd blow up and then it's all forgotten. Except with some people who bothered him all the time. In that case it wasn't holding a grudge, it was annoying him too many times.

RA: Did you like doing "Pecos Bill"?

I thought it was mediocre.

RA: Did you do "Johnny Appleseed" as well?

Yes. I got a kick out of doing his guardian angel who was a kind of soppy old character. I did "Appleseed", too, pretty much, but that was kind of a nothing character. I didn't enjoy the picture. I remember Ken Darby did the music and Walt had some criticism about that music. Darby said, "Well, that's a good cross section of one man's opinion!" The next day he was gone!

You *could* talk back to Walt. I talked back to him all the time. He respected me. He had a thing about musicians, though—an awful lot of these guys brought it on themselves. Ollie Wallace was one. I liked him very much—but he was such a funny egomaniac.

RA: So when the features were on again, were you glad to get back to them?

Oh, yes, I should say so. Yes, because I'd spent my time on those education and propaganda films like *Education for Death*.

But still, for me *Cinderella* wasn't much of a picture because I did only the King and the Duke.

RA: You did all that scene with the bouncing bed?

No. The funny thing...we had a director at the time by the name of Clyde Geronimi. He shouldn't have been a director at all. He was an animator. We used to cover for him all the time because it was easier that way. We just wanted to make a good picture. I didn't give a damn about him.

I always remember...he worked on one of the sequences in *Fantasia*. The first time he heard Beethoven when he knew it was Beethoven, he said: "I don't know about this Beethoven; he ain't no Tchaikowsky!"

Norm Ferguson did the bed sequence in *Cinderella*. Geronimi was the director on it. "Fergy" had been directing for a long time, and Walt got sour on him as a director and put him back into animation. And animation had passed him by. He was an awfully nice guy, but he'd kinda had it, I guess.

Geronimi came to me and wanted me to do all this stuff over again. He didn't even want to give Norman credit for it. I wouldn't do it. I wouldn't have any part of it. He wanted me to do it all over again, and then he wanted to take all the scenes away from him [Norman] and make them my scenes. I just wouldn't do that.

RA: Tell us about your work on *Alice in Wonderland*.

I did Alice herself. Again, you know, it was a group effort. I started a character out—a couple of hundred feet—so you could say, "This is the character," and I'd move on to another one. Other people would then take over, and that's what happened with Alice. I only did about a fourth, maybe a third of the *Alice* footage, but other people like Bill Justice would do the rest. I looked at the Tenniel illustrations. They're very good, but they wouldn't have been good for that picture.

I think Alice herself is successful in the scenes where I start her out, like in the interview with the caterpillar. I think I also did her with the flamingo in the croquet game.

RA: Did you do her in the English garden at the beginning, where she lies down among the daisies?

No, I did not. The sequence is all right, but Alice didn't satisfy me in it.

RA: So you had humans in *Cinderella* and *Alice*, and then you were given Wendy in *Peter Pan*.

I'd get these things that nobody else wanted to do. Uninteresting. Alice was rather uninteresting, too. Also, I didn't enjoy working with things that used live action as reference material, and later on I was able to get away from it entirely. I was just adamant about it. I talked about it so much that I guess they left me alone.

Alice has an awfully weak story but a lot of charm to it.

RA: Did you like Carroll's original book?

Yes, but then again, you don't have any substance to get your teeth into at all. And the picture doesn't have any more than that. The book is charming because it is so nonsensical. But all you had as motivation, from the time she went down the rabbit hole, was trying to get home. That's all you had to go on. That's not very much. You never took her seriously.

RA: You do feel sorry for her in the woods.

Yes, I did that part, too. But you know when you have live-action help, it's anything but creative.

We had multiple directors in those days—each guy would have a sequence and try and outdo all the rest of them. Thank God we had Walt because none of these guys were directors, really. They were all kinda helping to keep things together, you know. Walt was the director.

Dr M: That's what Jim Algar said yesterday. He said one day Walt came in and said to him, "Okay, you're now directing this...."

Yes. Jimmy had an awful lot of responsibility because he was directing those *True-Life Adventures* and Walt would leave him pretty much alone. I was never alone with those guys in the sweat box. I imagine that Jimmy had a lot more free rein than any of the other directors. On the animated things Walt had to be so damned close to them.

Another thing about feature-length animation is completely different from live-action features. For instance, when the director of the Disney Channel program *Family Album* came up to do that thing about me, he filmed about three hundred minutes of stuff and what was he going to use? About fifteen minutes. But animation is so incredibly expensive you couldn't do it that way. The stuff had to be all pre-cut, all pre-planned, so that you knew exactly where you were going to have close-ups or long shots, everything.

RA: Did the little girl who voiced Alice, Kathryn Beaumont, also do the live action?

Yes, she did. Sweet little girl.

RA: Did you shoot the live action?

No. We had a camera crew. We had a terrible time with getting permission to do anything because of unions.

R: What about *Peter Pan*?

Bobby Driscoll did the live action. He was a nice little boy, but he had an absolutely terrible mother. She was one of these Hollywood mothers who was a pusher. Damn shame. Nice little kid. I just loved him in *Song of the South*. Real cute little boy and you loved him.

RA: Did you do Wendy and Peter as well?

Yes. I did her brothers, too. I did an awful lot of that stuff. I designed the characters and helped guys to do them. It was frustrating for me because I'd start things off and someone else would do them, so that I can't point to anything in these pictures and say it was mine.

Then later on I had more to do. For instance, in *Jungle Book*, I did practically all of the tiger and a big chunk of Bagheera.

RA: You looked at film for the tiger, but on *Peter Pan* did you go to Victorian book illustrations? Did you go to the library?

Yes, but we also had a lot of the story people involved. In fact, a hell of a lot of people were involved. It was a group effort. I did a lot of drawings and helped Frank Thomas out with the *Peter Pan* costume. You had something to do with the design of it whether you wanted to or not.

Dr M: Yesterday, Lee Blair showed us some watercolors that Mary Blair had done for *Alice* and *Peter Pan*. Were those just to give the ideas of the colors?

Yes.

RA: Styling?

Yes, but styling more than the colors. Her stuff had an awful lot of charm, not just so much for the colors but the way it was drawn and designed.

Dr M: So you already had those when you began working? They were hanging up somewhere?

Yes. For the most part.

RA: And you had model sheets for the characters from the Story Department?

No. Not really. We'd have them, but the design of most of these characters would come from me; at least for the characters that I was involved with, and I was [involved] with most of them. So I probably had more to do with the design of characters than maybe anybody in the place, including the Model Department.

Dr M: Did you do those model sheets where they have six poses of the character?

A great many of them. I didn't do the sheets, but in later years we didn't make model sheets, per se. They'd take a lot of drawings from my animation and make a model sheet of those. It was much better that way because the model department, well, they couldn't really draw that well anyway. They were good artists but...I don't know. When something gets into animation, it forces itself into a different design. Especially heads. Faces. Because to articulate them, there were certain things that just didn't work.

Dr M: That's true with the beginning of *Snow White*. They had a lot of problems articulating her.

Yes. That's just inability to draw. The judgment of how *not* to draw something. Somebody would say, "How do you draw Pinocchio looking straight down on him?" And I'd say, "You don't draw him that way." Because it looks like hell.

RA: You had the Prince in *Sleeping Beauty*. Once again you get landed with the difficult part.

The hard characters to do are those that don't do anything. The Prince is one of those. The hero doesn't show relation, despair, anger on anything. Heroes are in the middle of everything. That's what made Johnny Appleseed such an uninteresting character. The hardest thing to do in animation is nothing.

RA: Can I take you back to *Bambi* and ask if you knew the Italian artist Rico Le Brun?

I'm sure he was French![1] We had life classes and he would conduct. He was quite good, and we got a lot out of those classes. They made you think; they made you animal conscious; they made you skeleton conscious.

RA: What about Eyvind Earle?

He was a damned good colorist. I didn't like *Sleeping Beauty* from its design standpoint, though. I didn't like Eyvind's designs, really. They were too two-dimensional and too many sharp edges and that sort of thing. But his color—beautiful.

The whole picture was heavy, and was around at a very unfortunate time. Disneyland opened in 1955, and that was Walt's baby, you know. He threw himself into everything. He knew everything about that park. His engineers were saying that this was too high and the water wouldn't flow and he would say, "The hell it is." He knew more about the contour of the ground than they did. He was really, really into it.

It was almost impossible to get him into story meetings. He was a genius in so many ways, this man. He was overwhelming.

RA: What did you do on *101 Dalmatians*?

I did Pongo and Perdita. Roger and Perdita, in fact, mostly. I did a lot of the dogs but they were also done by quite a few people. Marc Davis did Cruella.

---

1 In reality, Le Brun was Italian.

I took live action on most of the stuff but didn't pay much attention to it. You've got a lot of lazy people in the business. You shoot live action and they'll follow it blindly because it's a lot easier than thinking.

RA: Is it Walt who's saying, "Right down from *Snow White* to *Sleeping Beauty*, we must have them more realistic"?

Yes, that's right.

RA: The more realistic they get, the more wooden....

Realism isn't wooden. It isn't that. It's the people you have doing it. I just didn't follow live action that closely. Later on I was fortunate to have my own way in these things and didn't use live action at all with Ector and Kay in *Sword in the Stone*. They're a lot better. And on *The Rescuers* I didn't use any live action on Medusa.

I've worked awfully hard and have studied how people move, and you don't have to use reference then. Observation of people, movement, what muscles are involved, balance, weight. It's something you just learn. I could animate an animal from how it *has* to move.

RA: Did you study with Don Graham?

Oh, yes. It was stimulating. I remember I had fights with Don Graham all the time. Over perspective and an ellipse. I respected him.

R: What about other artists that you've liked?

My God, I've practically worshipped Picasso. Although there's a great deal of his work that I don't care for, that I think is ugly, he absolutely overwhelms me. This is a real great, great genius.

RA: You've talked a lot about Walt. You obviously stood up to him when you disagreed with him. Were you unusual in that?

Yes. The reason I could—I'm not particularly brave—was I could do something that Walt was no good at. He was a lousy cartoonist. He couldn't really draw at all. He was an absolutely wonderfully creative man, a wonderful storyman and a fountain of ideas. Some were lousy, some were good—most of them were good. As a storyman, my God, he was the best in the world. Even as a director. Jimmy Algar couldn't stand up to him, and Jimmy was both.

RA: Did he welcome criticism?

Yes, but he was hard to change if he'd made up his mind.

On the Fairy Godmother, he wanted a tall, stately fairy godmother. He had a preconception of it. I told him, "It'd be awfully good, Walt, if maybe you had a little roly-poly godmother...." He didn't agree with me. I did a compromise.

You had to be fairly honest. If you were a yes man, you could say yes one day to a stupid idea and get your ass in a sling the next for saying so.

What he didn't like was someone making wisecracks in a story meeting. On *Jungle Book*, he had so many ideas. He got on this thing about Mowgli growing up into puberty and being lured by civilization. I made a crack and he gave me the dirtiest look. He didn't like it.

© 2004 Robin Allan

Harper Goff (1911–1993)

Interviewed by Robin Allan on July 7, 1985

Harper Goff was born on March 16, 1911, in Fort Collins, Colorado. His first meeting with Walt Disney happened in 1951 at the Bassett-Lowke Ltd. Train Shop in London, England. A brief discussion with Walt led Harper to work for Disney in Los Angeles.

Harper's accomplishments while working with Disney include creating the storyboards for *20,000 Leagues Under the Sea* and designing Captain Nemo's *Nautilus* submarine, which remains his greatest claim to Disney fame. He also did conceptual work on Main Street U.S.A, the Haunted Mansion, the Jungle Cruise, and various other projects throughout Disneyland. He later contributed to the EPCOT Center project. He was also a banjo player for the Firehouse Five Plus Two band.

Harper Goff died on March 3, 1993, and was posthumously named a Disney Legend that same year.

Robin conducted this interview at Harper's home in Studio City, California, as part of his research for what would become the book *Walt Disney and Europe* (Indiana University Press, 1999). Harper was a very kind and interesting man who spoke frankly of his period of work with Disney.

....

Robin Allan: Could you tell us first about your youth?

Harper Goff: I was born at Fort Collins, Colorado, and came to California at the age of nine. I had Scotch and Irish parentage way back. My dad owned papers in Colorado, but in the First World War he couldn't get paper and couldn't expand. He was quite sick when we moved. I had to support my mother, and began working at 14 sweeping the street for a store in Santa Ana. I got up early, did the next store's sidewalk, and I was making about $26 a week. I already knew I wanted to be an artist and I did show-cards for stores.

When the Depression came, I did very badly. But just before this, my art teacher, Miss Egge, had shown a woman my work. She presented it to Chouinard and I got a scholarship. I swept out after morning classes, and after afternoon classes I swept up for the night and early in the morning. I also got little jobs as an artist during the Depression.

I literally starved, and sent all pennies back to my mother. I lived in a shack in downtown L.A. There was a little Indian tailor there, a Hindu who made suits. He said, "Are you hungry? I have mulligatawny stew going constantly (I smelled his stew). I have been busy doing over furs and I'm in work—so eat!"

There was also the owner of the Stendhal Gallery where they sold fine chocolate. He saw how hungry I was, so he invited rich widows, asking them in to bring me a bit of pot luck.

Around that time I saw the silent movie of *20,000 Leagues Under the Sea* (1916), made by the Williamson Brothers down in Florida. I loved the special effects movies like *The Isle of Lost Souls* and *The Lost World*. I made little theatres for myself, and I did my own movies after seeing these films.

Roosevelt had ten percent of public works available for art projects, murals, etc. I got thirty-five dollars a week doing a ships mural for the Customs Office of the Government. A man called Steinberg saw it and said "I'll get you a job at Warner Bros. Studio." I said, "I have no portfolio". He said "Go!" I went. I got into Warner in 1935. And I wrote to mother saying that I would start at $100 a week. Today, there's a van at Warner full of my pictures. I worked as Art Director for a while at Warner. Our sound system picked up the aircraft noise, so everything had to be recorded inside.

RA: How did you come to work for Disney?

In 1951, I went to Europe. I was interested in model trains and I visited the famous Bassett-Lowke model railway shop. They had an antique steam toy locomotive of 1907 at 11 guineas that caught my eye and which I decided to buy. But another man had already called and wanted it. He was coming back at 4:30. I came back, too. The salesman said, "The man is here." It was Walt Disney. He wanted my engine.... [A brief discussion with Walt followed.]

Later that day, Bill Walsh rang me from the hotel Dorchester. "Could you go to the Ambassador's tonight to meet Walt?" he said. I told him that I had nothing to wear. Bill said, "We'll all go in our ordinary clothes."

That evening Walt asked, "Where have I seen your work?" I had done illustrations for *Esquire* magazine, and Walt said, "Ah, yes, that's where I've seen it. I've been cutting out your stuff for our library. Now I have a project," says Walt, "and if I get any encouragement to go ahead, I'd like you to work for me." [Editor's note: The project was named *20,000 Leagues Under the Sea* and was to be a short subject about fish and whales using brand-new technologies. It bore no relation with Jules Verne's novel at the time, aside from the title.] Well, I was doing well at Warner for 12 to 13 years, and had a good pension. But it was so imaginative that I signed. Everything I did from there on pertained to the studio.

RA: At the same time you were also involved with the "Disneylandia" miniatures, weren't you?

Yes. Walt was starting to think about Audio-Animatronics. He had a large collection of clockwork toys. This was a little Disney town with miniatures. When I started working on that project I had a secret office and we couldn't talk. I learned later that Don DaGradi was also working secretly—because of espionage worries—and we were integrated.

RA: How did you start working on the full-length version of *20,000 Leagues Under the Sea*?

At that time, Walt went to England for a long time to do English films and stayed over for weeks. I worked alone. I was sent to the oceanography museum, as Walt wanted me to get the light breaking up on water and to get a size scale for the *20,000 Leagues* short subject. [In parallel, I began doing Jules Verne-type drawings on my own while working on the short subject.] I made a machine for when Captain Nemo's men take the men out of the water and then bring them back on the ship and show them Nemo's own aquarium.

[I wanted to convince Walt to produce a movie based on Jules Verne's work.] So I added more storyboards. He came back from England. I rang his secretary and said that I didn't know what to do about the project. A while later, Walt was sitting in my office with his eyebrow look, and said, "When the cat's away, the mice will play. You know that we don't make live-action pictures here in Burbank. We don't have the plant, the facilities."

The next day Walt was there again. "You know," he said, "I was talking to my daughter and asked her to read the book and I asked her who to cast. I had thought of Charles Boyer to be Nemo. Both my daughters thought of Kirk Douglas...but *I'm* not going to do *20,000 Leagues*. I'm going to do *The Great Locomotive Chase* and I've got the man who wrote it to come out and meet you. We'll do ARI [Audience Research] on both." So we did research and we got all the exhibitors' consensus that *20,000 Leagues* would be more popular. "You s.o.b.," he said, "they all want *20,000*."

I became the big duck in a little pond—the big stage tank—I had to do it all. Walt said, "What the hell! Is all this plywood?" He wasn't yet ready for live action.

RA: How did you design the *Nautilus*?

How did I get the *Nautilus* look? Well, firstly I wanted the authentic look. I hated movies that had boats that didn't look like real boats. Once I was on the *Oregon*, used in the Spanish-American War, and it had a real feel—the captain's table, the cabinet work, the brass fittings, and a map on the wall. That's what I was looking for.

And secondly, I was crazy about the Firth of Forth tubular railway bridge in Scotland. As a child, I had had stereo pictures of it, a strip of the making of the bridge. I had the idea of Nemo's ship having a tubular structure, neutrally buoyant. But that was written out because of the story. Nemo made the *Nautilus* out of steel plates.

He had a specimen case of amphora like in a French museum—the top of the glass case had to be at an angle and the French realized this. Accounts of the sightings of the Nautilus said that it was a sea monster, so I got to thinking of a menacing water creature, with the shape a mixture of the manta (benign), the shark with its menace and dorsal fin, and the alligator, lying there near the surface with its eyes open.

Dick Fleischer, the director, and Earl Felton, the screenwriter, worked on it for a year. We got a simple story and cut out minor episodes. James Mason was cool about it. Walt came to me and said, "How do you like James Mason?" I equivocated, and he said, "You'll have to like him because I've got him." Mason was very professional.

You had to get Paul Lukas to dub Paul Lukas as he swallowed key words. Peter Lorre was very good, Kirk Douglas fantastic.

RA: Can you tell us about your experience working on Disneyland?

On my first visit I went round on a jeep, barred by ditches. I worked twelve hours a day, and Walt came down on Sundays to okay things.

Walt wanted and got the right people. I was working on the Jungle Ride, solely in charge of it, costs, everything.

One day I was late for a meeting and Dolores (Disney's secretary) told me that Walt was in the meeting. I overheard them say before I went in, "One thing you ought to know, Walt, Harper is way over budget on the waterfall."

Walt did not answer. I went into the meeting. Walt said nothing.

Later, I went back and told Walt that I had overheard the dialogue. Walt said "Is it true? You were wheeling and dealing pretty good, and I felt if you were in trouble you'd come to me." I told him that we could save money on electricity through hydraulics. He would really back you. We also had trouble with the water level, with the special clay from the desert which was to seal the level. Another thing I did was watch over the false ceiling and floor for the *Mark Twain* to make the railing safe for people.

RA: I believe that you saw Walt almost break down once while the park was under construction.

[Yes. Walt was almost alone and high up on the central scaffolding that was built in the middle of the park.] It was nothing but a sea of drains and ditches and nothing above ground. "I have half of the money spent," he said "and *nothing* to show for it." He said this with tears in his eyes. "Nothing!" And he was not a fearful man.

RA: How did you leave Disney?

Flossie, my wife, had organized a three-month vacation for us, for by this time I had back trouble. Walt said, "If you leave, you're fired. I'm grooming you." But by this time I was very sick. Flossie threw hysterics. So I left.

Later, I got work with Jack Webb [creator of the TV show *Dragnet*]. Walt thought I was unethical in leaving him. I also worked on the Unisphere at New York, so he saw me as a competitor.

But later, Walt asked me to work on the planning of Walt Disney World on World Showcase to show America's heritage. I was forgiven.

© 2004 Robin Allan

Joyce Carlson (1923–2008)

Interviewed by Jim Korkis in 1998 and 2000

Joyce Carlson joined the Walt Disney Studio in 1944 as a "traffic girl", which meant she delivered mail to the various departments among other responsibilities.

She soon transferred to the Ink and Paint department and spent sixteen years inking cels on many of the classic Disney animated features, including *The Three Caballeros*, *Victory Through Air Power*, *Cinderella*, *Peter Pan*, *Sleeping Beauty*, and others. In 1962, Joyce moved over to Walt Disney Imagineering, then known by the acronym WED, as a model maker for the 1964 World's Fair pavilions where she worked closely with Mary Blair and Marc Davis on *It's A Small World*.

Joyce was the natural choice to help bring *It's A Small World* from the World's Fair to Disneyland. She eventually was also the key person involved in bringing the attraction to the Magic Kingdom at Walt Disney World in 1971, and later Tokyo Disneyland in 1983.

For several years, Joyce was based in Florida, where she was known affectionately as "Miss Joyce-y." She was the resident expert on *It's A Small World* as well as maintaining other Audio-Animatronics figures and working on a little bit of everything, including helping select the colors of the carousel horses at the Magic Kingdom. Joyce was the one who developed new figures for *It's A Small World*, including children representing Israel and Korea.

When she retired in February 2000, she was given a window on the Walt Disney World Main Street that read: "Dolls by Miss Joyce. Dollmaker for the World. Shops in New York, California, Florida, Japan and Paris. Owner and Founder Joyce Carlson."

In 2000, Joyce was made a Disney Legend. She passed away on January 2, 2008.

The following is a selection from interviews Jim Korkis did with Joyce in 1998 and in 2000 at Walt Disney World, as well as some bits and pieces of additional conversations Jim has had with her.

....

Jim Korkis: I think probably we need to start with where you were born and some of the background before you came to Disney.

Joyce Carlson: Sure. Well, I was born in Racine, Wisconsin, on March

16, 1923, and in 1938 my mother and father decided to leave Wisconsin to move to California. That was before the War, and we decided we wanted to move to maybe San Diego. But when my mother saw those sailor boys down there she said, "We're not living here," so we moved to Santa Monica, and that's where I lived starting in 1938.

JK: Did you have any background training in art either in high school or college?

I went to Santa Monica High School and graduated there in 1943. Rolly Crump went there later. I used to do some carvings with a pen knife. Things like that. I'd go down to Beverly Hills and go into the back alleys and rummage through the stuff that stationery stores and such had thrown away and make things out of that. I wanted to create, but there were no jobs around for just creating. I love to make things, so it was a natural thing for me.

JK: Was your family artistically inclined?

There's a lot of talent on my mother's side, so I must get a little of it from them. Her four brothers upholstered furniture, and she used to do things like drapes and all that. She was artistic in that way.

JK: You joined the Studio in 1944. What made you decide to come to Disney?

A girl I went to high school with moved to Burbank, and she worked for Disney. She kept saying, "Why don't you come out to Disney?" I said, "I'm not a cartoonist. I want to do industrial designing. I don't want to work for Disney." And my mother kept telling me to work for Disney, and my friend kept pushing me to come on out. She worked in Traffic there, and I finally said, "Okay."

JK: So you went into Traffic as well?

I spent some time doing a little ABC product like working on walkie-talkies, drilling, machinery, that sort of thing. But I quickly got tired of that, and went into Traffic.

JK: We often hear people refer to "Traffic" jobs at Disney, but some people don't understand what that job entailed.

Well, in the main animation building there were four floors. Walt was up on the top. Each floor had its own Traffic Department. The animators would need pencils, brushes, or coffee, so we would run down and pick them up and take it to them in their rooms. In Traffic, you delivered things, ran errands, brought guests up to Walt's office, delivered mail.

That sort of thing. I got into trouble delivering mail because I would drop it right on the big boys' desks. I went right through the door and dumped it on the desk. I didn't realize you were supposed to put it up front with the secretaries. So I didn't last too long in Traffic. (Laughs) I lasted about six months.

JK: And from there you moved to Ink and Paint?

Well, my boss Ben Mosley and his wife, Violet, said, "Bring some of your work in. They're hiring in Ink and Paint." She was Cockney and I could never quite understand what she was saying. They were running the Traffic Department. I thought, "Ink and Paint? What am I going to do over there?" I had a few carvings, but I didn't think that would impress them. So I went home and sketched about six drawings with pen and ink. Ben took my work over to Grace Bailey. I don't think they'd hire me today if I showed them to you. Grace was just taking Ink and Paint over. Ben took my work over and I guess he put in a good word for me, and they decided that maybe I'd be good for inking. Grace kept saying, "You're only18?" and I said, "No, I'm 21." She was suspicious and kept saying, "You look 18," and I said, "Oh, I'll bring my birth certificate tomorrow." I was hired for Ink and Paint. They programmed me for two weeks' practice, and after two weeks they put me on production. We were doing a lot of the war insignias and the shorts for the army and training films. That was fun.

JK: Some people often confuse Ink and Paint. Inking was a separate craft than painting.

Oh, yes, we had three quarters of inkers upstairs, and two or three quarters of painters. And of course we had checkers, final checkers. The checkers were in the quarters where the inkers were. Each quarter in inking had about 20 girls. And then we had two checkers up front, and then we had a supervisor and an assistant supervisor that was in each quarter.

JK: So you were never a painter?

I was never a painter, even though I could paint. Inkers did all the line work in pen and ink. You did pen and ink of the characters and mud and water if you were lucky.

JK: Lucky?

Yes, because there was a quota. And if you were given mud and water, that went so quickly you'd be on top of the average. I was always close to the bottom because they gave me mostly the main characters. Some

of the figures had twelve colors, and you had to change your pen points
and mix your colors, and that took a little time. Sometimes an hour to
do just one cel. I was worried about being below the average, but my
supervisor said, "Don't worry about the average. Just do it right."

**JK: Didn't you even have charts where they had examples of ink
lines, because you had to match the lines?**

You'd call for work and they'd give you six drawings of whatever feature
you're on, like *Cinderella*. I always seemed to get the main character, and
as I mentioned, there's about twelve colors on each drawing, each cel.
And that's what takes time. I had to watch the girl that was before me
ink the line because there's a fine line, a medium line, and a heavy line,
so you had to follow her lines so it runs smoothly. Otherwise, it'd jump,
and that's what we did. You had to match what the other girls were doing.

JK: Did you use a quill pen or did you use a brush, or both?

They had quill. I've still got some of my old pen holders and pens, and
they still have ink on them. [Laughs]

JK: But you still had fun?

Oh, yes, I had a lot of fun in the corridors. There were four corridors of
inkers and three corridors of painters, as I recall.

**JK: I understand that the Ink Department was on the second
floor, Paint was on the bottom floor, but there was a tunnel
connecting the building to the animation building?**

Yeah, there was a hallway and you could go down underneath. There was
a printing office down there that was printing out these little things in
ditto or mimeo, I guess. Sometimes we'd help out the guy down there
and he might give us a lift into Hollywood. I lived out in Santa Monica,
and in those days we all hitched rides into Hollywood to catch a streetcar
or a bus to get home. I remember some times walking down the middle
of the street at 1:00 in the morning in the dark. They had all the lights
out because of the War. It was great. No one bothered you. But I wouldn't
walk to the mailbox by myself today. So when it was raining, it was kinda
nice, you could use this tunnel to get from one building to another and
you didn't get all wet. Yeah, we had that underground passage.

**JK: Now, there was quite a separation between male and female
employees, right?**

We'd get a talking to from the boss, "You're not supposed to fraternize
with the animators," but we'd go over and see what they were working

on. We'd have fun doing that. We were known as the "nunnery". All women. Just women. We had one fella, Lloyd, who punched the cels. He was sort of feminine himself, so he fit in with the girls. But he was the only fella that was in Ink and Paint. He was a nice fella, we enjoyed Lloyd. But he doesn't count. He wouldn't have looked good in a nun's habit. But we'd sneak over to see the animators and maybe run into Walt on the elevator over there.

JK: And then what would happen?

Oh, Walt was very warm and friendly. If he wasn't talking to someone else, he'd talk to you. It was such a pleasure to see him in the halls. Everybody admired Walt. He knew what he wanted. And we all wanted to help create his dream. He was a man you looked up to.

JK: I also understand in those days the color keys were sometimes done on ditto and sometimes on a cel?

In color models, they got the drawings of the characters in the feature and they would put color to the pencil lines and then they'd write down the color of the areas on the cels.

JK: Now, you started in 1944, which was toward the end of the War. Did you have any security-clearance problems that you went through?

Oh, yes, we all had to wear our badges to get into the studio, and there was a lot of security. I was away for a little time and when I came back, they were taking them away from us. They said, "You don't have to wear them anymore." I wish I had known that was happening because I would have said "I lost my badge," and then kept it. They took all the badges to the front office. When they took our badges away, we could just drive in, and didn't have to go through the tight security they had during the war.

JK: Did you ever meet any of the military officers?

Oh, no, they were over in the animation building. They never visited the nunnery.

JK: You stayed in Ink and Paint for about 16 years?

Pushed a pen around for 16 years. No wonder I can't see today. (Laughs)

JK: What was a typical day like for an inker?

Well, we had a commissary and that was it for an eating place. And we'd come in and go up the corridor. We all had our own desks. There were about two desks next to you, and there were about 20 girls. Sometimes it'd get real cold in there, y'know, and you can't move your hands, so we couldn't ink. So we'd call the air conditioning man and he'd come up and get it nice and warm. We were happy at the end. The temperature was pretty good there. In the middle it was pretty good, but up front it was too hot. So everybody complained, you know how girls are. (Laughs) But we'd sit down and we'd have our 5-field cels, 6-1/2-field cels and 3-pan cels. We'd have to roll them up and put them on our boards.

JK: For those who are unfamiliar with that term, field is basically the area that the camera will film.

We had our work or we'd call into the supervisor if we were running out of work. My supervisor nicknamed me "Hot Shot".

JK: Why'd you get nicknamed "Hot Shot"?

I had red hair and freckles. I've still got the freckles. There was a popular comic strip called *Terry and the Pirates*, and one of the characters was a pilot with freckles. His name was "Hot Shot." If you needed more work, you held up a little sign. One day my supervisor said, "Okay, Hot Shot," and that name stuck with me for quite a while. I even had a sign that said "Hot Shot". One day, I accidentally left it near the waste basket, and I guess the people cleaning up thought I wanted it tossed away, so they did. If I saw any of the gals today, they'd probably still call me "Hot Shot".

To come back to our typical day: we'd call in for work and get maybe six drawings, depending what character you were on. We'd have to order paint from the Paint Lab, and we had a "dummy" in the hall. The Paint Lab was right down below, and they would put the paints on it and send them up. Then the color models would get their paints and we would get ours—black ink and certain colors that we needed for the cels we were doing. We'd have to fill out a form and get our paints that way.

You had to be careful with the inking. You had to use your entire arm, not just your fingers. You had lines that tapered off. It was really hard on your eyes.

JK: Did Walt ever visit you girls in the Ink Department?

Oh, he used to come over. He used to walk through or bring guests through to see what we were working on. But otherwise, that was it. He was always very friendly to us.

JK: Did he ever give you any presents to show his appreciation?

At Christmas time, we'd have a little party and he'd bring little compacts, face powder, nylons, cosmetics, and he'd go around to all the girls, and you could pick what you wanted. Merry Christmas! [Laughs]

JK: How would you describe the "Walt Disney" you knew?

Well, Walt was…special. You saw him coming and he was someone you could look up to and you wanted to please, do a good job for him, help fulfill his dreams. It was exciting—you'd get on the elevator with Walt, and he'd talk to everybody. It was wonderful, you'd just admire him so. We miss Walt. I miss Walt.

JK: Do you have a favorite story of meeting Walt?

One time in 1954, one of the little Russian girls in Ink and Paint gave me a box of candy and this little metal red toy car. I had just gotten a 1954 Ford. On this little toy car, you'd pull the handle and it scooted across the floor. So I was walking out to my car and here comes Walt. He was going over to Camera, and he passed me. Then, all of a sudden he stopped, and he came back and said, "What do you have there?" And I said, "Oh, Walt, I got a new car, so someone got me some candy and this little toy." So he picked it up and looked at it carefully, and he said, "Oh, that's nice." Then he went back to walking over to the Camera Department. That little car has fond memories because he admired something I had.

When you were doing the shows, he'd always be there. When we'd do our reviews for our scenes that were inked and painted that day, he'd be up there in our box. We'd always have to fill out a paper, what we thought of the color or if it wasn't inked too well. But he'd read them carefully. He was always out in the hall. He'd read them later, but he was always collecting them. He wanted to know what we thought. But now when I see all our films on television, like *Lady and the Tramp*, and all those great, beautiful features, the inking was beautiful. Of course, we use Xerox now, which is quick, but it's also nice in its way.

JK: Did you go to Disneyland when it opened in 1955?

Oh yeah, I still have my ticket, opening day ticket. (Laughs)

JK: What was opening day like?

We were all invited. There were so many people that weren't invited. Oh, it was terrible. It was a hot day. Walt was real thrilled, you know. He had Art Linkletter and Bob Cummings, and he was so excited about the show. But it was dusty, and there was still a lot of dirt around.

The only thing I rode was the carrousel. That was the only thing I was able to get on, and I had a Coke, that was my day. Oh, it was fun! We had a good time that day.

JK: Had you ever seen anything like that? I know that there's Long Beach Pike and everything out there.

No, it wasn't anything like that. By Vons market, they'd had some ponies. I used to take my nieces there. That's all they had, little ponies to ride, or a train that went around. I know that Walt used to go on the corner of Fairfax and Beverly and they had a Ferris wheel and he'd take his girls there, Diane and Sharon, on Sundays. So I guess that's when he dreamed up Disneyland. He said, "The girls are having fun and I'm not," and he's sitting there watching, dreaming up Disneyland.

JK: Obviously, you've been back to Disneyland, so you've had a chance to ride more than the carrousel?

Oh yes, I had to go back and ride *It's a Small World* many times.

JK: In 1961, when they went into xerography and they fired the entire Ink Department, what did you do?

Well, they showed me the door. All us inkers left, of course. Grace Bailey asked if I wanted to transfer over to Painting, and I told her it just wasn't my cup of tea. But one thing about inking is you can always get a job on the outside in the ink and paint services. I used to do that for a little extra money overtime and working Saturdays and Sundays with Slim Miles' Ink and Paint Services because studios would all call for the former Disney ink and paint girls and try to get us to do some work when they were pressed on deadlines. I remember one time earning enough so I could take a little trip to San Francisco.

JK: It was around this time that you made the move over to WED, right?

Rolly Crump, big Jack Ferges, and a few others were over there at WED. Rolly was working on some toys, and I said, "Oh, I want to work with you." So he said, "Okay," but he had to get approval from Mary Blair and somebody else. There were three of us girls who started in the Model Shop at WED at the same time. Glendra was one. She was married to a count or something, and she had the longest nails and they were great for gluing little things. Dick Irvine hired the three of us and wanted to see what we could do with the model for the General Electric Carousel of Progress.

We were doing the little furniture for the set pieces, little ladders and refrigerators, all old fashioned. We didn't have all the necessities to work with, you know. So for the show models, Leota Toombs' father gave her some chewing gum, wires, and a bag of earrings. They were one-of-a-kind things. We'd use everything off those earrings—the little jewels, the back pieces of the earrings for the little hinges on the refrigerator, and such. We didn't have a lot of supplies, just string and wire and paper and cardboard to work with. Secretaries started bringing in bags of their old jewelry so we could use it. That was fun. We didn't know they were testing us to see what we could do. When we finished, Walt used to bring guests to show them the projects and he'd say, "Do you believe that this whole set was built on earrings?" and everybody would go, "Earrings?!" Anyway, I guess they liked it because I got moved over to work on Small World.

JK: WED was not on the Disney studio property?

We were off over by the San Bernardino Road, yeah. It was a little place and they had a carpenter's shop in the back, but we didn't have too much room in there. That's where we did all the toys for Small World, for the New York World's Fair. That was fun. Walt used to come in with Rolly Crump early in the morning and we'd have the coffee wagon back there and he'd have a cup of coffee and go sit on Rolly's desk. He'd come sit with Rolly and talk about the toys, Rolly's toy shop. Then all the big boys would come in and snatch him away. (Laughs) But he'd come in all the time and talk to everybody, even Christmastime he would show up. They would say, "I think Walt's coming to the party," and they'd say, "No, he isn't going to come," but he did. He'd always show up! He'd talk to the traffic boys and tell which project, like the Haunted Mansion, was coming up, and they'd stand there listening to Walt. He used to be so excited telling them about all the new projects. He was wonderful, and the boys were just so thrilled.

Rolly's cubicle was right near me. One time, Walt was walking around the model shop. Rolly had found an old Shell gas pump out in some field somewhere. It was full of cobwebs and stuff. He had it standing in his cubicle. Rolly had some idea for it; he was very talented. Anyway, Walt came by me around lunchtime and was looking at what I was doing and then wandered over to Rolly's place and stopped and looked at the gas pump. I could hear him say, "What the hell is that?" And I said, "That belongs to Rolly." Walt said, "Oh, okay." Rolly came back, and I said, "Walt was admiring your pump over there." Rolly removed it out of there and I never saw it again. He must have taken it home. Walt never missed a trick. He always noticed everything that was different.

JK: Didn't Roy O. Disney come by sometimes, too?

That was when I was working on a zebra for the Jungle Cruise. I never painted a zebra in my life, full scale you know. I thought all the stripes were the same, but they're not. There's about four different species of zebras. So I picked up all these books from the library, and I said to Marc Davis, "Which zebra do you want?" And he said "That one." So

I mixed the colors and painted that zebra. I was just finishing it up and putting the eyelashes down and putting the mane in and the tail. We put wire in the lashes because in the park the birds would come and pull out the hair for their nests, so I had to put in wire so they would stay on the zebra. We had this horse hair and a needle you stick into the skin, and Walt came by and looked at the zebra and says, "Oh, that's a good-looking animal." And I said "Oh, thank you Walt." Then Roy came by later, and Roy was balding and said, "Joyce, could you put a little hair on the top of my head like the zebra and the tail?" And I said, "Sure, but it'll smart a little." So he walked away. Later on he came by and said, "I changed my mind. If it smarts, I don't want it. I'll just stay the way I am." (Laughs). He was fun and very sweet. Roy was very nice. He didn't come around often, but Walt was always checking out what we were working on.

JK: When you mentioned you worked on the toys in Small World, that refers not only to the props but to the little children figures as well?

Yes, those Audio-Animatronics figures with the rubber heads. For the World's Fair version of Small World, just about everything was made out of Styrofoam, and then we added things like plastic flowers, jewelry, and glitter. I went all over Los Angeles to find these things cheaply at places similar to a Pick'n Save. It was a shock when I came to Florida because they didn't have all these places and I couldn't find the things I needed.

JK: You worked very closely with Mary Blair.

Mary was very friendly and very artistic. She had a lot of glasses. She used to have a lot of different colored contact lenses as well. She used to wear green or blue or any color to go with the outfit she was wearing that day. I'd watch her put them in, and I thought, "I wouldn't want to wear those." Maybe that affected her colors. Her colors were always bright. She used theatrical gels and cut them up and put them on top of her artwork. I had to match the colors she picked, and that was a problem because those colors didn't exist with the paints we had. I had to go and get some of the paints from the Ink and Paint Department and mix them in with our paint, and they didn't always mix well. It was like painting with mud.

When I worked with her on the mural in the Walt Disney World Contemporary Hotel, it was a little easier because the tile work wasn't as bright like Small World but it was still tough. I would finally get what she wanted, but it took time. Mary painted very flat and it wasn't very dimensional. We often had to cut pieces of Styrofoam for her and let her move them around. She wasn't always happy how her artwork got translated to animation, but she was happy with the finished product of Small World, I think. Of course, other hands were involved as well. Mary would let us put our ideas together, and she'd pick things we'd do and put them in the show. I created a cardboard giraffe for the African scene, and Mary loved it and put it in. We'd always be changing characters and adding things. It was what I was looking for when I was in Ink and Paint—something creative.

Mary's paintings are all flat. She started to learn a little dimension toward the end. But her work is charming. I only have one book of hers, the children's Little Golden Book that she did. That's what we used to help us understand her designs afterwards. She was a wonderful talent.

JK: And you also worked with Rolly Crump.

All the girls in the Ink and Paint Department liked Rolly. Rolly was in Animation across the way. The girls would say, "You see that new fellow in Animation? His name is Rolly Crump." He came out of the animation building one day and we all ran to the window to see him. He had muscles and was in good shape because he was training and working out and running. The girls would say, "That's Rolly." And I said, "He's good looking but he's too young for me." And they all said, "Well, not for us!" So everyone got to know Rolly.

He liked me. He was married and had two girls and a boy, Chris, who is now a designer. Walt always called him "Orland." I don't know where Walt got that name, and I don't think Rolly knows, either. He'd say, "My name is Rolly." Walt still called him "Orland" all the time.

JK: And you also worked with Marc Davis on *Small World*.

Marc would come by and he had a cigarette holder this long [extends her hand far from her mouth]. He'd come in and the girls would be painting some of the Small World figures, and he would bump into them and get paint on his slacks. We'd spend time trying to scrub the paint off of them. His wife Alice used to complain, "His pants are always full of paint!" He loved being with us. We had a lot of artists in the Model Shop and everybody contributed.

JK: They were three very forceful artists.

In the European scene, Rolly designed the chess people. Mary asked me to put jewels on the king and queen. Marc said not to put them on. I was caught in the middle. Apparently, they had a loud discussion about it. Mary came to me and apologized for me being put in the middle. Then she said to put the jewels on. I listened to Mary and didn't hear anything else. Everybody had a say about the ride. I really loved working with all of them. I used to admire Mary from afar when I was in Ink and Paint, and I would see her and Walt walking around the studio. And Marc was wonderful. He really knew what he was doing

JK: Did you get to go to the World's Fair in 1964?

Oh, yeah. It was hot! Well, all these executives were going over to New York from the main studio, and we were the ones that worked on all the shows and put them together and we weren't. So Mary Blair finally talked to Walt and said: "Their noses are being bent and you better send them over." So we got to go to New York for ten days. It was great. It was August and it was very hot. They put us in Queens, right by Shea Stadium. There were ten of us for ten days, and Walt gave us each three hundred dollars cash spending money. Boy, that was quite a bit in 1964. I even had money when I came back. Mary Blair lived out on Long Island with her husband Lee. They had a sailing sloop and took us out on the water. It was raining and it was like a movie. We were drinking and the boat was moving back and forth like this. Glendra's dress was shrinking because of the rain. Her sleeves were shrinking. Oh, my, we had a lot of fun.

JK: What was the guests' reaction to these rides?

We were given our VIP badges and the hostesses would take us through the lines to get on certain rides. We'd see these lines of people waiting for Small World or a lot of the shows, and I'd want to go by quickly because it's hot and little kids are crying and they would walk us right into the shows. Of course, we had to fill out a folder every day. We had to write up what we thought of the ride and the ideas we thought were great, and if we had any ideas for them. We had a certain number of things we had to see each day. We had to write every night like homework. Walt would read those folders when we brought them back home to California. That's what we did every day, but we would be escorted by all the guests waiting in line. It was just terrible. That was the only thing that bothered me. But, oh, we saw all the shows, and not just Disney shows. That was quite an experience. The guests loved all the Disney rides, especially Small World.

JK: Most of these shows were brought back to Disneyland?

We didn't bring back Rolly's Tower of the Four Winds because it was out of scale. They made the pipes much larger, and it would have taken up too much room at Disneyland. So we left it there. When we brought back Small World, we repainted, freshened it up, and put it in the show at Disneyland. We had slapped it together for New York, so we had to do some redesigning. We expanded it and improved on the characters.

JK: There is only one character who is unhappy in *Small World*.

Yes, the little clown in the basket under the balloon. He is holding a sign saying, "Help!" Mary designed that and I made it. He wants to get out of the basket but we can't let him get out. (Laughs) He's frowning because he's floating away and wants to come back down with all the others.

JK: You must have heard that song quite a bit.

Every day. All day we'd hear that song over and over and over. They gave us the album. I never opened it. Never cracked the seal. I guess now it is a collector's item and I should put it up for sale.

JK: After the World's Fair, what projects were you assigned to?

Well, let's see...I used to do a lot of inking for Marc Davis for some of the shows that were coming into Disneyland, and for Claude Coats, too. So the inking experiences had come in handy for some of the set pieces.

JK: What was your day like at WED?

I'd come in around 8:00 am. We were all on different projects. If there was a deadline to have a model ready, we'd all jump to that model to put in bushes and trees to help finish it up and be ready for the meeting. I remember Claude Coats wasn't always happy with the changes we would make on the model, because he felt it was a gorgeous model to begin with and we were changing things. We'd go for a martini lunch and then come back. We'd work on the weekends or holidays if they needed to get something quick. My supervisor would ask, "Going anywhere over the holidays? Could you help?"

JK: Tell me more about those martini lunches!

When we worked in Glendale, we didn't have a cafeteria at WED. We had these machines for soup and coffee. So we'd go out for lunch every day and have martinis. Lee and Mary Blair would have two or three, but Glendra would have at least three or four.

It was a place called Checks Cashed. Herb Ryman would come by. I don't remember Rolly going there. He probably went somewhere else for a beer.

There was sawdust on the floor. We played pool in there. The hamburgers were forty cents and they were this big [indicates a large size] and they were great hamburgers. So we'd order a hamburger and a martini. Every day we'd go in there and have martinis, but we still got our job done. I don't know how I lived through that.

JK: Did you work on all the Small World attractions?

The Disneyland one is still my favorite. I worked on that. I worked on the one for Walt Disney World. They bring out the toys and figures from Disneyland out here to Florida and I work on them. I rarely get to Disneyland when I go out to California nowadays because I have so much to do. Japan was going to put it in Tokyo Disneyland, so they asked quite a few of us in the Model Shop to move out to Florida to work on the show. Most turned down the offer. Tokyo wanted the Small World we had here in Florida because each one is different. There were only two of us who said we'd go to Florida.

They sent me out here in January 1981 to work on the toys and figures, over in Central Shops; we were all in one room. There was hardly any room to do all the painting and such. Even in the middle of the room, we were standing on tables and painting. They sent three Japanese over to get in the mood of painting and working with Styrofoam and mixing the right colors. I think they are all executives now. I went to Tokyo for ten months and put in the show. We had the best time.

The one in Paris is a little different. It's got new scenes, backgrounds, different toys, and all. So it is an entirely different show than the one here in Florida. They are all a little different. Though I've always liked the European scene with the balloon kids, can-can dancers, and Eiffel Tower—they're all my kids. I couldn't choose. You might say I've got a big family in Small World.

JK: You've also worked on other projects.

I worked on the carrousel out here at Walt Disney World. I helped pick the colors and painted a little bit. The horses in France are beautiful, too. I don't read so much any more, but if there's a certain project coming up, I'll read about it and learn about what they want me to do. Like America Sings. I wish we had that show here in Florida. That was a good show. I did all the hats. Seventy-two hats. Then my boss says, "They're gonna make another set of hats," and I say "There goes another year!" [Laughs]

JK: Some of those critters ended up in Splash Mountain. Are they wearing your hats?

Some are, I guess. But they shouldn't be out in the rain, because they're just glue and water. They'll go limp as an old rag. But the hats were all made of felt, glue, and water. Marc Davis was the one who sketched them all, and I had to paint them. You go down to California to get one of these hoods, where they make hats. You can't get the color of the hood, because Marc dreams up these colors, you know. Real nice, so I had to mix the colors. After they were hard and dried, I had like a bake shop outside the door and put them out there like cement. So I'd mix the colors, paint the hats, put the brim and crown together, and go to Pick'n Save to get all these flowers to put on the hats, and Marc just loved them.

Shirley Temple even came through, and she was the most wonderful person. She made you feel as if you'd known her for 100 years. She'd go over and pick up one of the straw hats I'd finished, and she put it on her head and said, "This reminds me of a neighbor who used to wear a hat like this when I was a little girl." And I thought, "Oh, that's cute." It didn't go with her dress at all, but she looked cute in it. She came back twice in one year and she was terrific. You just felt so at ease. But they introduced her as "Shirley Black" and I knew it was Shirley Temple. But anyway, she came back twice to look at the hats again. She was wonderful. I have some fond memories of the day I met her.

JK: Did you have any project that you really liked or you found exceptionally difficult?

Well, the one I really liked was Small World with Rolly Crump and Mary Blair. We started off using rubber bands with the dolls. It was primitive, but we used sheer style. Then when we brought them back to Disneyland, we fixed them up a little better and put motors inside and improved the style. I loved Small World, all those toys. Of course, today all the countries want to be in our show and we don't have room. Mary designed it to have sections of the world like the Orient, and we thought that would work, but now they all want their own sections. We get lots of letters from guests. We got a lot of letters that in the goodbye scene we had spelled "Auf Wiedersehn" wrong. I guess we didn't know. It was spelled that way on the blueprints and we just followed the blueprints, but we were wrong. Sometimes people write and they are concerned about how their country is represented. We try to re-design and make people happy.

We thought we were only going to have one Small World and we ended up with four. Originally, Mary and I only bought enough material for one. We tried using authentic fabric for the countries, and it was hard to find even then. Today, it is even harder. We try to buy in bigger quantities now. We have cupboards filled with braid and stuff.

JK: I know you are in charge of maintaining the Small World attractions. Is it difficult?

Depending upon how active the toys are, if they turn their heads or raise their arms or something, it rubs against stuff. So we have them on a rotation system to pull them out for repair. If you put on a new arm, sometimes the costume no longer fits properly, so we have to work on the costuming. We use little doll eyes in the toys, so we have to be careful about the color of the eyes we are picking in regards to a particular country. The insides of the figures are different from the originals. The parts are larger now, or sometimes the arms stick out more or sometimes their little bottoms stick out too far. So we have to trim down the costumes. Sometimes companies go out of business and we have to find something else for a replacement. The bright colors fade and they don't do the rehabs like they used to. I will ride the ride and list if maybe one eye is stuck or the mouth isn't moving. I try to go through and list what needs immediate attention.

JK: You are officially retired now, right?

I officially retired in February 2000, but I still come in for four hours on Monday and four hours on Tuesday. Eight hours a week. I go over to the Central Shops and hang out with the artists. I used to hang out there all the time. The people are still creative and talented and so great to work with. There's a little of this and a little of that going on. That's one of the reasons I enjoy what I do. As long as I can come in every day and help out, I'll show up.

One thing these young kids learned from me is how to mix colors. They say, "You want me to put in some raw umber?" That's one of my secrets to perking up a color. When I retired, they gave me an Audio-Animatronics child figure from Small World that was made up to look like me, with a special costume and big glasses and a hat and a little badge saying "Joyce" on it. The badge is so small I can hardly read it. I am half Norwegian and half Lithuanian. I have it in the dining room under my big Mickey clock in the corner. So every time I come out of the kitchen, it is there staring at me and I wave to her and walk by. She is about three feet high. She is beautiful. I've got to find a special spot for her. I have received a lot of awards over the years, and I need to find a special place for those as well. I have a fifty-five-year pin with a sapphire in it. John Hench is the only one who has been around longer with the Company, so he got his pin first. I also have a pin with Mickey and a diamond for fifty years' service with the Disney Company.

JK: I know you were also called in to do special projects. I had heard you inked the little Mickey for one of the Ingersoll watches.

The watch changed so over the years. They've got so many of them, but then, at that time, they wanted this little Mickey. Of course, they would always give me the little stuff to ink. No wonder I can't see today. But I inked the Mickey. My boss said it was for Walt and I thought, "Why'd you say that?! Now my lines are going to be all wiggly!", and held my breath. They brought in this tiny cel of Mickey for me to ink. It seemed like the tiniest thing in the world, and they gave it to me because they said I did these things so well. They used that Mickey on one of the Ingersoll watches. Then they brought in one of these watches and opened it up, and I had to paint the little Mickey hands. Someone had painted them yellow, and I had to go and repaint them white, and then ink in all the little black lines. I couldn't do that today. I am lucky to see. They did give me a copy of the watch.

JK: Was Walt a workaholic?

Workaholic? Yeah, he was a workaholic. He was always coming up with ideas and working with the animators and people like Mary. Yeah, I could see him and Mary walking around the studio discussing a feature, and Mary would do all the backgrounds at that time. That was before Small World. He always worked with the animators and the storymen and then later the folks at the Model Shop all the time. Workaholic? Yes! [Laughs]

You know, when you saw Walt coming, you were so pleased to see him and wanted to do your job the best to make him happy. He'd talk to you, never condescend or act like he was something special. If you were on a special project, he'd come over and look at it and discuss it and want your ideas. You wanted to please him all the time. You wanted to put a smile on his face. He would come into the Model Shop and cough to sort of warn you. It was a smoker's cough because he smoked all the time, but I think he did that to let you know if you were working on something you weren't supposed to that you'd better put it away.

JK: Did you ever see Walt grumpy?

Yes, I did. In our Model Shop at WED, he was having a meeting with the big boys, and we had our desks all around the place and the model in the middle of the room. He was quite a smoker as I said, but anyway, when he'd come into a room, you could hear him coughing and once you heard that, you'd know to be on your toes and best behavior because here he comes! [Laughs] But anyway, he came in and all the "yes" men were around him and so he stood there and he was telling them what he wanted, and if they weren't agreeing or being as enthusiastic as he was or something, his voice got louder and louder and he wasn't happy with them. So, all of a sudden, they disappeared. But he got his way, I'm sure. [Laughs] That's the only time I ever saw him grumpy. He never hesitated to let them know if he wasn't happy. He came in quite often.

JK: What type of qualities do you think an Imaginer should have?

You have to be thinking of new ideas all the time, and if there's a new project coming up, sit down and discuss a lot of new ideas, and who you're going to work with and who can create this or that and put the show together. It's never a one-person project. It is always a team. A lot of talent, get them going and let them share a lot of ideas, and use the best ones. That was what Walt would do. I loved it because it was a creative area. Over the years, there seems to be a lot more paperwork for one thing. We need more areas to express our creativity.

JK: Anything you would have changed about your life, Joyce?

No, I wouldn't have changed a thing about my life. I always wanted to be in the creative end and I got my dream. I've still got lots of ideas and boxes and drawers filled with things and tools. Around Christmas, I get ideas and I make things out of Styrofoam. I love working with Styrofoam. I still have one of my pens from my ink-and-paint days where I can get any kind of line you want from thin to thick. I still get out into the parks. I still ride Small World.

I like to see the smiles on the kids and parents when they go through Small World. That's what Walt wanted...for people to be happy.

© 2004 Jim Korkis

Further Reading

Below you will find additional reading material that is indispensable for completing the portraits of all the artists interviewed in this book. We tried to select only those sources that give very in-depth knowledge or a different perspective on the artist's work and career.

Books and Articles

Rudy Ising

Russell Merritt and J.B. Kaufman, *Walt in Wonderland* (Edizioni Biblioteca dell' Imagine, 1992).

John Kenworthy, *The Hand Behind the Mouse: An Intimate Biography of Ub Iwerks* (Disney Editions, 2001).

Brian Burnes, Dan Viets and Robert W. Butler, *Walt Disney's Missouri* (Kansas City Star Books; 2002).

Dave Hand

David Hand, *Memoirs* (Martha Hand, 1986).

Bill Tytle

John Canemaker, *Vladimir Tytla Master Animator* (Katonah Museum of Art, 1994).

"Golden Age Animator Vladimir (Bill) Tytla" by Izzy Klein in *Cartoonist Profiles* number 17 (August 1970).

Ken Anderson

John Canemaker, *Before the Animation Begins* (Hyperion, 1996).

"Story Book Land with Ken Anderson" in *The "E" Ticket number 11* (Summer 1991).

"An Interview with Ken Anderson" in *The "E" Ticket number 13* (Summer 1992).

"An Interview with Ken Anderson" in *StoryboarD, The Art of Laughter* volume 2, number 4 (Aug./Sept. 1991).

Jack Hannah

"The Story of Jack Hannah" by Jim Korkis in *Persistence of Vision* number 8.

John Hench

John Hench, *Designing Disney* (Disney Editions, 2003).

"John Hench: An Other Kind of Reality" in *The "E" Ticket* number 11 (Winter 1993–94).

"Two Disney Artists" (Interviews with John Hench and Marc Davis) by Armand Eisen in *Crimmer's: The Harvard Journal of Pictorial Fiction* (Winter 1975).

"About Destino: Partners in Surrealism" by Jordan R. Young in *Comics Scene* number 18.

"A Disney Animator Looks Back" by Betsie Richman in *Disney News* volume 20, number 4 (September/November 1985).

"A Talk with John Hench" by Karen Cure in *Disney News* (Winter 1982–83).

"Living Treasures of Imagineering, Part 1" by Blair Howell in *Storyboard* (July/August 1988).

"Living Treasures of Imagineering, Part 2" by Blair Howell in *Storyboard* (September/October 1988).

Marc Davis

John Canemaker, *Walt Disney's Nine Old Men and the Art of Animation* (Hyperion, 2001).

"Two Disney Artists (Interviews with John Hench and Marc Davis)" by Armand Eisen in *Crimmer's: The Harvard Journal of Pictorial Fiction* (Winter 1975).

"Designing Disneyland with Marc Davis" in *The "E" Ticket* number 7 (Summer 1989).

"Marc Davis: His 'Haunting' Tale" in *The "E" Ticket* number 16 (Summer 1993).

"Animal Interactions by Marc Davis" in *The "E" Ticket* number 25 (Winter 1996).

"Marc Davis: A Pirates Sketchbook" in *The "E" Ticket* number 32 (Fall 1999).

"An Interview with Marc Davis" in *StoryboarD, The Art of Laughter* volume 2, number 6 (December 1991/January1992).

"That Old Black Magic" by Jamie Simons in *The Disney Channel Magazine* volume 11, number 3 (April/May 1993).

"A Toast to Marc Davis" by Charles Solomon and Kevin Markey in *Disney Magazine* (Fall 1992).

"Remembering Walt" column by Marc Davis in *Disney News* (Fall 1992).

Milt Kahl

John Canemaker, *Walt Disney's Nine Old Men and the Art of Animation* (Hyperion, 2001).

"Milt Kahl, an Animation Michelangelo" by Andreas Deja in *StoryboarD, The Art of Laughter* (June/July 1992).

Harper Goff

"An Interview with Harper Goff" in *The "E" Ticket* number 14 (Winter 1992–93).

"Remembering Walt column by Harper Goff" in *Disney News* (Summer 1986).

"Living Treasures of Imagineering, Part 1" by Blair Howell in *Storyboard* (July/August 1988).

"Living Treasures of Imagineering, Part 2" by Blair Howell in *Storyboard* (September/October 1988).

Magazines

Animation Blast

Cartoonist PROfiles

Disney News

Disney Magazine

Funnyworld

Hogan's Alley

Persistence of Vision

Storyboard

StoryboarD, The Art of Laughter

Tales from the Laughing Place

The Disney World

The "E" Ticket

Tomart's DISNEYANA Update

Twenty-Three

WD Eye

Websites and Blogs

Walt Disney Family Museum: www.waltdisney.com

Disney History Blog: www.disneybooks.blogspot.com

Disney Book and History Network: www.pizarro.net/didier

Disney History Institute: www.disneyhistoryinstitute.com

Michael Barrier: www.michaelbarrier.com

Andreas Deja: andreasdeja.blogspot.com

Animation Podcast: www.animationpodcast.com

Jim Hill Media: www.jimhillmedia.com

Cartoon Brew: www.cartoonbrew.com

Daveland: www.daveland.com

Animated Views: www.animatedviews.com

Blackwing Diaries: blackwingdiaries.blogspot.com

Mayerson on Animation: mayersononanimation.blogspot.com

Animation Animagic: www.animation-animagic.com

David Gerstein's Ramapith: ramapithblog.blogspot.com

Andreas Deja: andreasdeja.blogspot.com

Michael Peraza: michaelperaza.blogspot.com

Floyd Norman: floydnormancom.squarespace.com

Vance Gerry Memorial: vancegerry.blogspot.com

Harriet Burns: www.imagineerharriet.com/harriet

Claude Coats: www.claudecoats.com

Gustaf Tenggren: www.gustaftenggren.com

Hans Bacher: one1more2time3.wordpress.com

2719 Hyperion: 2719hyperion.blogspot.com

Disneyville: kayaozkaracalar3.blogspot.com

Kevin Kidney: miehana.blogspot.com

A Film L.A.: afilmla.blogspot.com

Jim Fanning's Tulgey Wood: jimattulgeywood.blogspot.com

Cartoon Cave (Pete Emslie): cartooncave.blogspot.com

Stuff from the Parks: matterhorn1959.blogspot.com

Gorillas Don't Blog: gorillasdontblog.blogspot.com

The Pickle Barrel: perkypickle.blogspot.com

Animation World Network: www.awn.com

Harry-Go-Round: www.harrymccracken.com

Michael Sporn: www.michaelspornanimation.com/splog

Animation Who and Where: animationwhoandwhere.blogspot.com

Disney Comics Mailing List: www.nafsk.se/pipermail/dcml

Alberto Becattini's Animators' List: www.alberto-s-pages.webnode.it

Acknowledgments

This project is clearly a collaborative effort and would never have gone off the ground without the critical support of Disney historians and enthusiasts.

Jim Korkis is the godfather of *Walt's People: Talking Disney with the Artists Who Knew Him*. He suggested the very concept of the series while providing two of his best interviews for volume 1.

Along with him, my heartfelt thanks go to the historians who allowed me to reproduce their interviews in this volume: Robin Allan, Paul F. Anderson, Michael Barrier, J.B. Kaufman, Alain Littaye, Mike Lyons, and John Province as well as Christine Tweedly and Jim Hill who helped transcribe the John Hench and Ken Anderson interviews, Bob Welbaum, who did the most precise editing job I have ever seen and the talented Pete Emslie, who designed the cover image for this volume.

I am also indebted to Donald Ault, Nancy Beiman, John Cawley, Becky Cline, Sébastien Durand, Maureen Furniss, Jud Hurd, Jerry Jenkins, Hans Kiesl, Andrew Leal, Josh Noah, Don Peri, Craig Richardson, Timo Ronkainen, Randy Scott, Germund Silvegren, Charles Solomon, and Dave Smith, who all contributed directly or indirectly to the project.

Finally, without the love, patience and help of my wife Rita it would have been difficult to find the energy to put together this first *Walt's People* volume in a timely fashion, in the middle of a major lifestyle change and a move to Madrid, Spain.

Contribute to Walt's People

The *Walt's People* series began in 2005, with the publication of the first edition of this volume. Since then, 12 additional volumes have been published, with the 14th scheduled for spring 2014. Theme Park Press began publishing the series with volume 13, and will re-release each previous volume during 2014, in both print and digital (Kindle) versions. The series will continue for as long as new or newly discovered interviews with Disney artists are available.

If you are aware of any such interviews published in an obscure fanzine, in a discontinued publication, or on a members-only website, or if you or your family have material written by or about a Disney artist in your possession, we'd love to hear from you. Please contact the editor, Didier Ghez:

didier.ghez@googlemail.com

About the Authors

Robin Allan was awarded his Doctorate of Arts by the University of Exeter, England, in 1994 for his thesis *Walt Disney and Europe: European Influences on the Feature Films of Walt Disney*. He then adapted his text to make it less academic, and the resulting book was published under the same title by John Libbey in 1999. To conduct his research, he was fortunate enough to stay for three months in the summer of 1985 with his friends Dr Richard and Mrs Marilyn Hulquist, who lived in Westwood, California. He pedalled 19 miles every day on Dick Hulquist's bicycle to the Disney Studios in Burbank. *Walt Disney and Europe* won the Norman McLaren/Evelyn Lambert Award for the best scholarly book on animation for the National Film Board of Canada in 2002.

Paul F. Anderson has spent well over half of his life researching, writing, and delving into the creative legacy of Walt Disney. As of this writing, he has done over 250 interviews. Feeling a need and a responsibility for his work to be shared with others, Paul started a historical journal devoted to the creative legacy of Walt Disney titled *Persistence of Vision*, for which he now serves as editor and publisher. In addition to conducting interviews, researching Disney history, writing in-depth examinations of Disney topics, and editing the magazine, Paul also finds time to travel across the United States to give lectures and talks on Disney. In 2000, he was invited to be an Adjunct Professor at Brigham Young University to teach a class on Walt Disney and American Culture through the American Studies program. He has authored several books, the most recent being *The Davy Crockett Craze*, which takes a scholarly look at the 1950s Disney cultural phenomenon. As the recognized authority on the later years and projects of Walt Disney's life, he worked for the Walt Disney Family Educational Foundation and wrote two essays for their CD-Rom on Walt Disney's life. He served as a historical consultant for the Disney family on the documentary film *Walt Disney: The Man Behind the Myth* and was also interviewed for the film. Currently, he is finishing up his magnum opus on Walt and World War II (a book-length piece to be published in *Persistence of Vision*).

Michael Barrier began interviewing people who worked for Walt Disney in 1969, when he was editing and publishing *Funnyworld*, the first serious magazine devoted to animation and comic art. He interviewed hundreds more before the publication in 1999 of his book *Hollywood Cartoons: American Animation in Its Golden Age* (Oxford University Press), a critical history of Disney and other Hollywood animation studios. He is now researching and writing a biography of Walt Disney for the University of California Press.

Didier Ghez has conducted Disney research since he was a teenager in the mid-80s. His articles about the parks, animation and vintage international Disneyana as well as his many interviews with Disney artists have appeared in such magazines as Persistence of Vision, Tomart's DISNEYANA Update, Animation Journal, Animation Magazine, StoryboarD, and Fantasyline. He is the co-author of the art book *Disneyland Paris: From Sketch to Reality*, runs The Disney Books Network web site, and serves as managing editor of the *Walt's People* series.

J.B. Kaufman is a film historian who has written extensively on the classic films of the Walt Disney Studio. In addition to numerous articles, he is co-author with Russell Merritt of *Walt in Wonderland: The Silent Films of Walt Disney* and *Walt Disney's Silly Symphonies: A Companion to the Classic Cartoon Series*. Kaufman is currently at work on his first solo book project, *South of the Border with Disney*.

Jim Korkis is an award-winning teacher, a professional actor and magician, and a published author with several books (including *The Vault of Walt* series and *The Book of Mouse*) and hundreds of magazine articles to his credit. He is an internationally recognized Disney historian and his original research on Disney heritage has been used by the Walt Disney Company for a variety of projects. He taught animation at the Disney Institute and animation history for interns at Disney Feature Animation Florida.

Alain Littaye is a frelance journalist specializing in theme parks-related subjects. He is the co-author and publisher of the art book *Disneyland Paris: From Sketch to Reality*.

Michael Lyons worked as a freelance journalist, covering animation history and the animation industry for numerous magazines and web sites, including *Disney Magazine, Cinefantastique*, and Animation World Network. During this time, Michael wrote over 200 articles and interviewed animators and filmmakers working at the major studios, as well as legends of the industry. Michael currently lives in Orlando, Florida, where he works for the Walt Disney World Resort.

John Province began his career as an animation and comic strip art collector, writer, historian, biographer, editor and archivist in 1965, when letters to Charles Schulz and Fred Harman resulted in receiving an original daily strip from each. His historical and interview assignments led him to associations with dozens of industry professionals from the golden age of comic strips, comic books and virtually every American animation studio that ever existed. Their career memories captured on tape for all time remain a very special facet of Province's collection. Province's interviews and articles have appeared in *Animato!*, *Hogan's Alley*, *The CFA-APA Journal* (which he also edited), *Sports Legends Digest*, *1506 Nix Nix*, and *Newsreel*, as well as NCS publications such as *Slice of Wry*, *The Cartoon!st*, and the *CAPS Digest*. In 2003, John Province became an evangelical Christian, and now devotes his meager talents to spreading the gospel of Jesus Christ. He remains forever grateful to a loving and merciful Creator for the many blessings received in this life.

George Sherman served as Publications Editor at Walt Disney Studios from 1961 until his untimely death in 1974 at the age of 45. His interview of Bill Tytla was originally published in the magazine *Cartoonist PROfiles*, number 7, from September 1970, and was edited by Jud Hurd, who kindly authorized its use in this book.

About the Publisher

Theme Park Press is the largest independent publisher of Disney and Disney-related pop culture books in the world.

Established in November 2012 by Bob McLain, Theme Park Press has released best-selling print and digital books about such topics as Disney films and animation, the Disney theme parks, Disney historical and cultural studies, park touring guides, autobiographies, fiction, and more.

For more information, and a list of forthcoming titles, please visit:

http://themeparkpress.com

More Books from Theme Park Press

To see all our books, visit ThemeParkPress.com